GLOUCESTER TO BRISTOL

INCLUDING THE BRANCHES TO NAILSWORTH, DURSLEY AND THORNBURY

Vic Mitchell and Keith Smith

MP Middleton Press

BRANCHES

Cover picture: No. 1064 is about to leave Berkeley Road for Gloucester on 5th July 1947. On the left are the lines from the Severn Bridge. (H.C.Casserley)

Published June 2004

ISBN 1 904474 35 7

© Middleton Press, 2004

Design	*Deborah Esher*
Cover Design	*David Pede*

Published by
> *Middleton Press*
> *Easebourne Lane*
> *Midhurst, West Sussex*
> *GU29 9AZ*

Tel: 01730 813169
Fax: 01730 812601
Email: info@middletonpress.co.uk
www.middletonpress.co.uk

Printed & bound by MPG Books Ltd, Bodmin, Cornwall

INDEX

ACKNOWLEDGEMENTS

We are grateful to many of those mentioned in the credits for their assistance and also to P.G.Barnes, W.R.Burton, C.L.Caddy, H.Cowan, L.Crosier, G.Croughton, P.Fear, F.Hornby, J.B.Horne, N.Langridge, B.Lewis, Mr D. & Dr S.Salter, M.Speck, N.Sprinks, G.T.V.Stacey, R.E.Toop and finally our ever helpful wives, Barbara Mitchell and Janet Smith.

I.   Railway Clearing House map for 1947.

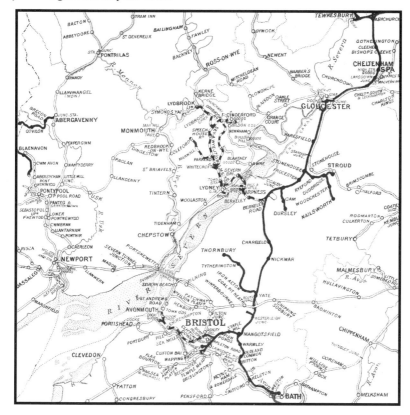

GEOGRAPHICAL SETTING

From the ancient trading centre of Gloucester the route is roughly parallel to the lower reaches of the River Severn, but several miles inland from it. The line climbs out of the valley initially and then takes an undulating course over Lower Lias Clays at the foot of the Cotswold Hills.

Three rivers are crossed, the Frome, the Cam and the Little Avon, before reaching an area of complex geology, which includes Coal Measures in the district south of Yate. Here, another and smaller River Frome is encountered.

The branch to Stroud and Nailsworth climbs into the Cotswolds, close to the northern River Frome and the Stroudwater Canal. The valley is narrow and deep for the final miles to Nailsworth. The Dursley branch has a similar but less dramatic environment.

The Thornbury branch is close to the southern River Frome and its northward tributary, the Ladden Brook, until reaching Tytherington. This is situated on the edge of an outcrop of Carboniferous Limestone, similar to that of the Mendips. Thus it is ideal for road making and a quarry provides considerable rail traffic. The branch required two tunnels to penetrate this mass to reach the terminus.

The now-closed part of the main line continued near collieries and brickworks into the northern suburbs of Bristol, descending steeply for the final three miles into the Avon Valley.

When the railway was opened, Bristol was a port of international stature and thus extensive joint wharfage was created. The city became an important commercial centre for diverse trades.

The maps are to the scale of 25ins to 1 mile with north at the top, unless otherwise indicated. From no. XXX onwards they are at 6ins to 1 mile scale and date from 1921-22.

II. Gradient profile showing the mileage from the Midland Railway's headquarters at Derby.

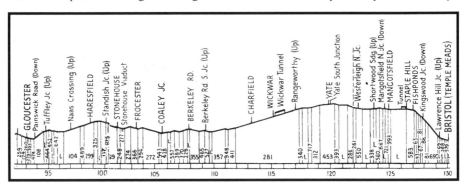

HISTORICAL BACKGROUND

The Cheltenham & Gloucester Railway was a 3ft 6ins gauge plateway which began operation in 1810. This tramway terminated at Gloucester Docks. The first conventional line in the area was the Birmingham & Gloucester Railway, which opened to passengers on 4th November 1840. It was standard gauge and became part of the Midland Railway on 7th May 1845.

The Great Western Railway between Bath and Bristol opened on 31st August 1840. It was broad gauge and was completed to London in June 1841. The Cheltenham & Great Western Union Railway was laid to the broad gauge of 7ft 0¼ins and was opened to Swindon on 8th July 1844, the same day as the Bristol & Gloucester Railway, which was of the same gauge. It was expected that both routes would become part of the GWR, but the Midland Railway offered a higher figure for the latter and took over its operation on 7th May 1845, together with the Birmingham & Gloucester. The GWR regretted its meanness for evermore.

The southern part of the route began differently. The Bristol & Gloucestershire Railway was authorised under an Act of 19th June 1828 to build a 4ft 8ins gauge railway between Bristol Harbour and Coalpit Heath, about nine miles north-east of the city itself, mainly for the conveyance of coal and building stone. Equine power was employed and the users provided their own wagons.

The Kennet & Avon Canal Company deemed that it would benefit if a branch was built south from the BGR at Mangotsfield to its waterway south of Bitton. The BGR branch, known as the Avon & Gloucestershire Railway, came into use early in 1831. The northern part of the BGR became operational during 1832, but it was to be 6th August 1835 before the section to Bristol was officially opened.

The Bristol & Gloucester Railway took over the Bristol & Gloucestershire Railway under an Act of 1st July 1839 and converted it to broad gauge. To enable the conveyance of coal to continue from the collieries to the River Avon, the original track was relaid between the new rails, north of Mangotsfield.

The South Wales Railway reached Gloucester on 19th September 1851 and it became part of the GWR in 1862. The MR was otherwise standard gauge and so it converted its line to Bristol on 22nd May 1854. On the same day, a new broad gauge line for GWR trains came into use; it was parallel to the MR tracks for seven miles south of Gloucester to Standish, where a junction had been situated until that time.

Four MR-operated branches followed. The Dursley & Midland Junction Railway opened on 13th September 1856, the Stonehouse & Nailsworth Railway came into use on 1st February 1867, Mangotsfield to Bath carried traffic from 4th August 1869 and the Yate to Thornbury branch followed on 2nd September 1872.

The GWR converted its lines in the Gloucester area to standard gauge on 26th May 1872 and it exercised running powers south to Yate from 27th January 1873, when Standish Junction came into being again.

The branch to Sharpness opened for goods traffic on 2nd August 1875, passenger trains following 12 months later. The Stroud branch carried goods from 16th November 1885 and passengers from 2nd July 1886.

A junction west of Fishponds came into use on 1st October 1874, known as Kingswood Junction. It served the Clifton Joint Railway, which gave direct access to Avonmouth from 1877.

The final main line in the area was between Swindon and the Severn Tunnel via Badminton. It was opened by the GWR in 1903 and was connected to the MR on 9th March 1908, near Westerleigh.

The GWR exercised its right to run over the MR north of Yate, following the completion of its Stratford upon Avon to Cheltenham line in 1906. From 1908, two weekday trains between Birmingham and Bristol travelled this way and completed their journeys via Filton. They did not call at intermediate stations on the MR route.

The GWR also used the 20 miles north of Yate for trains crossing the Severn Bridge, when the Severn Tunnel was closed for repairs.

The MR became part of the London Midland & Scottish Railway (LMS) on 1st January 1923, which mostly became the London Midland Region of British Railways upon nationalisation in 1948. Our route and its branches were transferred to the Western Region on 1st February 1958.

The first two branches in the table below lost passenger trains on the dates given, but the official closure dates were 8th June 1949.

The main line was closed south of Yate South Junction on 18th January 1970, although a short section is presently in use for freight. Passenger services were diverted onto the 1903 route and now run via Bristol Parkway. Coal trains to Bath ran from Yate, the Fishponds line closing completely. Part of the Thornbury branch was reopened on 3rd July 1972 for stone traffic from Tytherington.

As a consequence of privatisation, trains on the route were operated by Virgin CrossCountry from 9th March 1997 and also by Wales & West from 13th October 1996. The latter was part of Prism Rail plc and was rebranded Wessex Trains in 2001.

Closures took place as follows:

Branch	Passengers	Freight
Stroud	16th June 1947	1st June 1966
Nailsworth	16th June 1947	1st June 1966
Dursley	10th September 1962	13th July 1970
Sharpness	2nd November 1964	Open
Thornbury	19th June 1944	3rd September 1967
Bath	7th March 1966	28th May 1971

PASSENGER SERVICES

Down trains (southbound) running on at least five days per week are considered in this section. The table indicates the number of trains calling at both Gloucester and Bristol in sample years.

	Expresses		Stopping trains	
	Weekdays	Sundays	Weekdays	Sundays
1850	-	-	6	3
1869	5	2	5	2
1889	8	3	6	2
1909	11	3	6	2
1929	10	6	6	2
1949	9	7	6	2
1969	15	8	-	-
1989	19	15	-	-
2004	19	12	-	-

Expresses between Gloucester and Bath are excluded. These began in 1910 and mostly ran to Bournemouth via the Somerset & Dorset line. They were more numerous in the Summer, but were largely discontinued during the war periods. The name "Pines Express" was introduced in 1927 for the Manchester-Bournemouth service, but this and all such through trains came to an end in 1962.

The long distance services via Bristol reached their zenith in the 1950s, with around 15 extras running overnight on Fridays and during Saturdays. A number of such trains bypassed Gloucester and are therefore not shown in the table.

Nailsworth Branch

The weekdays only service comprised four trains in 1869, seven in 1890, nine in 1909, seven in 1929 and eight in 1946. In some years, there was an additional working between Nailsworth and Stroud, sometimes two.

Stroud Branch

There were connections at Dudbridge with most Nailsworth trains and a few timetables showed some extra trips between Stroud and Stonehouse only.

Dursley Branch

A weekdays service of six trains was provided in the first and final decades of the line. For much of the 1930s and 40s, there were seven or eight trips, usually lasting nine minutes.

Thornbury Branch

A sparse service of two return journeys was offered initially. This was soon increased to three, a figure that was maintained until closure. However, four trains were shown in some years, often in one direction only. Like the other branches, there was no Sunday service.

NAILSWORTH BRANCH. Midland.

Miles	Fares. 1st clss s. d.	2nd clss s. d.	gov s. d.	Up.	Week Days. 1&2 clss mrn	1&2 gov a	1&2 clss mrn	1&2 gov b
—	....	....	....	**Nailsworth** ....dep	7 40	9 35	1145	5 25
1½	0 4	0 3	0 1½	Woodchester	7 45	9 40	1150	5 30
3	0 7	0 5	0 3	Dudbridge fr Stroud	7 49	9 44	1154	5 36
4¼	0 9	0 7	0 4	Ryeford ......[170	7 54	9 49	1159	5 43
5¾	1 0	0 9	0 5½	**Stonehouse 169**, arr	8 0	9 55	12 5	5 50
34¼	6 0	4 6	2 9½	169 BRISTOL ....arr	9 40	1155	2 25	7 30
14¾	2 8	1 9	1 2½	170 GLOUCESTER.. ,,	8 25	1026	1235	6 20
73	12 6	9 6	5 11	171 BIRMINGHAM. ,,	1117	1 5	3 20	9 40

	Week Days. mrn	c	mrn	Saturdays only. aft	aft
New Street Station, 168 BIRMINGHAM dp	....	6 50	9 55	....	3 35
169 GLOUCESTER.. ,,	8 40	1010	1253	3 0	5 52
170 BRISTOL .... ,,	....	8 45	1110	1 50	4e35
Down.	1&2 mrn	1&2 gov	1&2 aft	aft	1&2 gov
Stonehouse ....dep	9 5	1040	1 20	3 30	6 30
Ryeford...........	9 10	1046	1 25	3 35	6 35
Dudbridge fr Stroud	9 15	1053	1 30	3 40	6 42
Woodchester	9 20	11 0	1 35	3 45	6 45
Nailsworth ... arr	9 25	1110	1 40	3 50	6 50

a 3rd class to Bristol and intermediate Stations. **b** 3rd class to Gloucester, Cheltenham, Worcester, and Birmingham. **c** 3rd class from Birmingham, Worcester, Cheltenham, and Gloucester. *e* 3rd class from Bristol and intermediate Stations.

June 1869

NAILSWORTH, STROUD, and STONEHOUSE.

Miles		Week Days only. mrn	mrn	mrn	mrn	mrn	aft	aft	aft	aft
	Nailsworth ....dep	7 35	832	920	10 0	....	145	3 22	4 43	7 5
1½	Woodchester.......	7 40	836	924	10 3	....	149	3 26	4 47	7 9
2¼	Dudbridge .....arr.	7 45	840	928	10 8	....	153	3 30	4 51	713
—	Dudbridge ...dep.	7 52	846	...	....	....	...	3 39	....	...
4½	**Stroud G** 72 arr.	7 55	849	...	....	....	...	3 42	....	...
	dep.	7 37	...	930	....	1020	145	3 30	4 45	...
—	Dudbridge ...arr.	7 40	...	933	....	....	148	3 33	4 48	...
—	Dudbridge .....dep.	7 48	...	934	10 9	....	156	3 36	4 55	715
4¼	Ryeford ..**656, 660**	7 52	...	938	1012	....	2 0	3 40	4 59	719
5¾	**Stonehouse F**..arr.	7 56	...	941	1016	1027	2 4	3 44	5 3	723

Miles		Week Days only. mrn	mrn	mrn	mrn	mrn	aft	aft	aft	aft	aft
	Eastington Road, **Stonehouse** ....dep.	...	8 30	...	10 0	1055	2 29	4 5	520	621	7 52
1½	Ryeford	...	8 34	...	10 4	1059	2 33	4 9	524	625	7 56
2½	Dudbridge .....arr.	...	8 38	...	10 8	11 3	2 38	4 13	528	629	8 0
—	Dudbridge....dep.	...	8 46	...	10 9	11 7	2 40	4 15	529	...	8 1
3½	**Stroud G** 73 arr.	...	8 49	...	1012	1110	2 43	4 18	532	...	8 4
	dep.	8 5	....	930	....	....	....	4 8	....	...	8 12
—	Dudbridge ....arr.	8 8	....	933	....	....	....	4 11	....	...	8 15
—	Dudbridge......dep.	812	8 40	936	....	11 4	2 42	4 18	...	630	8 20
4½	Woodchester........	817	8 45	941	....	11 9	2 47	4 23	...	636	8 25
5¾	**Nailsworth** .....arr.	821	8 49	945	....	1113	2 52	4 27	...	640	8 29

F Eastington Road: nearly 1 mile to Burdett Road Station. **G** Cheapside: about ¼ mile from Russell Street Station.

July 1929

DURSLEY and COALEY.

Miles		Week Days only. mrn	mrn	mrn	aft	aft	S	aft	aft
	Dursley ....dep.	7 40	10 5	1126	2 0	3 27	4 14	5 47	7 20
1¼	Cam.....................	7 45	1010	1131	2 5	3 32	4 19	5 52	7 25
2½	**Coaley 656, 660**.....arr.	7 49	1014	1135	2 9	3 36	4 24	5 56	7 29

Miles		Week Days only. mrn	mrn	mrn	aft	X	S	aft	aft
	Coaley ....dep.	8 43	1047	1145	2 28	4 5	4 27	6 25	7 45
1¼	Cam	8 48	1052	1150	2 33	4 10	4 32	6 30	7 50
2½	**Dursley**.........arr.	8 52	1056	1154	2 37	4 14	4 37	6 34	7 54

S Saturdays only. **X** Runs 5 minutes *earlier* on Saturdays.

July 1929

YATE and THORNBURY.

Miles from Yate.		Week Days only. mrn		aft		aft			
	Temple Meads 660 BRISTOL.....dep.	9P28	....	2 30	....	6P20	....	....	....
	660 BATH (Qn. Sq.) "	8 43	....	2U10	....	5 30	....	....	....
	656 GLOUCESTER.. "	7 50	....	1 53	....	5 46	....	....	....
	Yate ....dep.	9 58	....	3 22	....	6 57	....	....	....
2	**Iron Acton**..........	10 5	....	3 28	....	7 3	....	....	....
5¼	**Tytherington**.......	1012	....	3 37	....	7 10	....	....	....
7½	**Thornbury** ....arr.	1017	....	3 43	....	7 15	...	....	....

Miles		Week Days only. mrn	mrn		a	aft			
	Thornbury .....dep.	8P0	10 40	....	2 30	4P50	....	....	....
2¼	Tytherington........	8 6	10 45	....	2 36	4 55	....	....	....
5½	Iron **Acton**..........	8 14	10 53	....	2 46	5 5	....	....	....
7½	Yate C 656, 660 arr.	8 19	10 58	....	2 51	5 10	....	....	....
34¼	660 GLOUCESTER. arr.	1052	12 9	....	4 18	6 33	....	....	....
22¾	656 BATH (Qn. Sq.) "	9 31	12 2	....	3 46	6 12	....	....	....
17¾	656 BRISTOL (T.M.) "	8 55	11 35	....	3 28	5 48	....	....	....

NOTES.

a Runs on the second Wednesday in the month, Thornbury Cattle Market Day.
C Station for Chipping Sodbury (1¾ miles).
P Thro' Trains between Bristol and Thornbury.
U Departs at 2 25 aft. on Sats.

July 1929

YATE and THORNBURY

Mls. from Yate		Week Days only mrn		aft	aft	
	Temple Meads, **660** BRISTOL......dep.	7U50	..	1 20	630	..
	660 BATH .... "	7 32	..	12 22	542	..
	656 GLOUCESTER.. "	7 45	..	12 42	545	..
	Yate.............dep	9 10	..	4 5	715	..
2	Iron Acton...........	9 19	..	4 11	721	..
5¼	**Tytherington**	9 27	..	4 20	729	..
7½	**Thornbury**.......arr.	9 32	..	4 26	734	..

Miles		Week Days only mrn	E	S	aft	
	Thornbury......dep.	8 11	9 45	11 25	4 40	..
2¼	Tytherington	8 17	9 51	11 31	4 46	..
5½	Iron Acton...........	8 25	9 59	11 39	4 54	..
7½	**Yate B 656, 660** arr.	8 30	10 5	11 44	4 59	..
34¼	**660** GLOUCESTER.. arr.	10 47	2 49	1 11	6 49	..
22¾	**656** BATH	9 50	4 5	4 5	6 36	..
17¾	**656** BRISTOL (T.M.) "	9 28	2 9	2. 9	5R52	..

B Station for Chipping Sodbury (1¾ miles)
E Except Saturdays.
R Bristol (St. Philip's)
S Saturdays only
U Passengers can dep. Bristol (St. Philip's) 8 20 mrn.

January 1944

DURSLEY and COALEY

WEEK DAYS ONLY (Second class only)

Miles		am	am	am	S pm	S pm	pm	pm	pm
—	**Dursley** ... ... dep	6 35	7 35	9 55	1210	1 55	4 15	5 55	7 5
1¼	Cam.....................	6 39	7 39	9 59	1215	1 59	4 20	5 59	7 9
2½	**Coaley** ... . arr	6 44	7 44	10 4	1219	2 4	4 24	6 4	7 14

Miles		am	am	S pm	S pm	pm	pm	pm
—	**Coaley** .. .. dep	7 0	8 25	1235	2 20	4 40	6 25	7 40
1¼	Cam.....................	7 4	8 29	1239	2 24	4 44	6 29	7 44
2½	**Dursley** .. .. arr	7 9	8 34	1244	2 29	4 49	6 34	7 49

S Saturdays only

February 1961

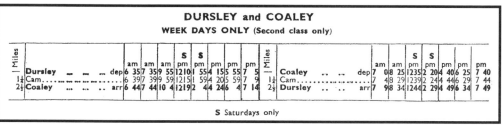

GLOUCESTER
The Evolution

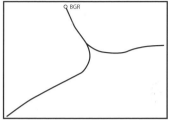

a.　　From 8th July 1844, trains from the south ran into the Birmingham & Gloucester's 1840 station. Those from Swindon were operated by the GWR and those from Bristol by Stothert, Slaughter & Co., on behalf of the Bristol & Gloucester. The two BGRs became MR property in 1845.

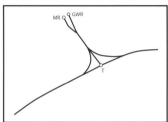

b.　　The GWR built its own terminus adjacent to that of the MR. In 1847, it added a link to permit direct running between London and Cheltenham. A "T" junction was laid on it to allow through coaches for Gloucester to be provided, by means of a turntable.

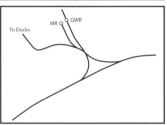

c.　　"T" Station was closed on 19th September 1851, after which date all GWR trains used the station of the South Wales Railway, which opened that day. A branch (top left) was opened to Gloucester Docks in 1848, this following the route of the tramway, which continued to run across the main lines of both companies until its removal in 1861.

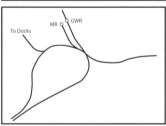

d.　　This plan existed from 22nd May 1854, when the MR converted the Bristol line to standard gauge and created the Tuffley Loop. The GWR removed its Cheltenham Loop when it too became standard gauge in the area in 1872.

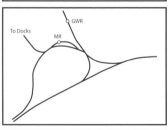

e.　　The next major change was on 12th April 1896, when the MR closed its terminus and opened a new station on the Tuffley Loop, as shown. The Cheltenham Loop was relaid and opened for goods traffic on 25th November 1901 and for through passenger trains on 1st July 1908.

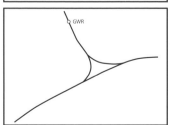

f.　　The final diagram shows the routes since 1st December 1975, when the Tuffley Loop and its station were taken out of use. There had been only one pair of tracks southwards since 8th September 1968. The lines to the docks were removed in 1971.

III.   The first passenger railway in the area was that of the Birmingham & Gloucester Railway which terminated in the goods yard between the two stations shown top left on this 1922 survey at 6 ins to 1 mile. The upper station is on the GWR South Wales line and was named "Central" from 17th September 1951. The lower one was "Eastgate" from that date until both were considered one station on 26th May 1968. The GWR engine shed is above the triangle, while the MR one is within it. A main road now bisects it at a high level. The route ownership is given on the lower part of the map. "T" Station became a dwelling and is marked as such. The sidings south of it became known as New Yard. The marshalling of Speedlink services was transferred here from Severn Tunnel Junction in October 1987.

1. The west facade of the city's first station was curiously imbalanced. The unimpressive structure became an embarrassment to the MR and it was replaced by the through station on 12th April 1896. The terminus had four roads, but only two platforms. The site was later used for carriage sidings. (LGRP/NRM)

2. The MR's new station had three through platforms and is seen from the south in about 1905. There was a bay platform at the north end and there were two goods lines beyond the right border of the picture. (M.Oakley coll.)

3.　　A panorama of the north end in 1923 includes (on the right) the bay platform, the footbridge over the goods yard to the GWR station and a grounded Pullman coach. (Stations UK)

4.　　The nearest stanchion in picture 2 appears again in this photo of 4-4-0 no. 41061 arriving with the 5.15pm Bristol to Birmingham on 8th September 1949. It is passing under Barton Street Junction box, which had 48 levers and a gate wheel for the nearby level crossing. (H.C.Casserley)

5.   The footbridge was a source of great annoyance to passengers, particularly when the range of tickets was limited at each booking office. The lack of side windows was another complaint. Gas lights were still in use in 1961. (Stations UK)

6.   The footbridge continues to the right of the 40-lever signal box, which lasted until 1968. No. D39 is working a Bristol to Newcastle service on 14th August 1962. The cathedral is also included. (J.Day)

7.   A northward view from 1962 features the up and down goods lines, which carried dock traffic in particular. The island platform was signalled for down trains only. There was a siding to a foundry on the site on the right for many years. (Stations UK)

8.   Barton Street Junction box ceased to serve as a block post on 26th May 1968, but continued to control the level crossing. There were four crossings on the half-mile long Tuffley Loop. No. 25152 is approaching the station with empty hoppers on 16th September 1975. Lifting barriers came into use on 3rd December 1960. (T.Heavyside)

9.   Seen on the same day is DMU no. B407 forming the 14.10 Cheltenham to Bristol. This area is now occupied by a B&Q car park. The line to the docks on the left was known as the High Orchard Branch and was in use until 1st October 1971. (T.Heavyside)

10.   Clearance on 11th May 1977 enables us to see the canopies on both sides of the station, together with the lantern roof over the booking hall. Closure had taken place on 1st December 1975. Only the island platform had been in use since 26th May 1968, it being numbered 2 and 3. (H.C.Casserley)

11.   East of the station is Horton Road Junction which is partly on the level crossing of the same name. The term "Tramway" was used for both until 26th May 1968, a legacy from the time that the 1810 Cheltenham & Gloucester Railway crossed main lines of different gauges here to reach the docks. The 1968 panel box is out of view to the right of no. D1029 which is hauling a mixed formation towards the station on 16th September 1975. No. 45057 is standing near the line from Cheltenham. (T.Heavyside)

12.   The former Central station was reduced to one passenger and one parcel platform, plus two through lines, in 1968. However, the main platform could accommodate 30 coaches and was divided into two parts on 8th March 1977, when the rebuilt station was officially opened. A down bay was numbered 3 for Chepstow trains and the parcels platform became No. 4. No. 45125 was working from Cardiff to Newcastle on 3rd November 1979. (T.Heavyside)

GLOUCESTER DOCKS

IV.   This overlaps the previous map
and has the High Orchard Branch at the
top. It follows the route of the 3ft 6ins
gauge tramway, which had been purchased
by the MR. The company laid standard
gauge track nearby in 1848 and prevented
the GWR having access to the east side of
the waterway. The docks had been opened
in 1810 and the Gloucester & Berkeley
Canal was completed in 1827. The lower
part of the map includes the New Docks
Branch, which was brought into use on
5th September 1898. The MR property
extended as far as the Timber Pond. The
GWR owned the other lines on that side
of the canal. The two systems were also
connected at Llanthony Bridge (top left).
Lower left is the 1913 line to the gasworks,
which had opened on this site in 1888.

13.　　No. 47506 is running north as it leaves The Park, shown top right on the map. The date is 14th February 1962. (M.A.N.Johnston)

14.　　About to enter The Park on its way to Eastgate station on the same day is 0-4-0T no. 41537, one of a small batch of 33-ton locomotives introduced by the MR in 1907. (M.A.N.Johnston)

15.　　Shunting the dock lines on 1st February 1962 was sister engine no. 41535. South of this location was the extensive works of the Gloucester Railway Carriage & Wagon Company, which generated much traffic on the High Orchard Branch. (M.A.N.Johnston)

16. Behind the camera in June 1962 is Bristol Road level crossing; on the right is the Atlas Engineering Works and at work in the distance is 0-4-0T no. 51535. The High Orchard line closed on 1st October 1971, after much track reduction in 1964. (W.Potter/ Kidderminster Railway Museum)

17. Hempsted Sidings were on the 1898 New Docks Branch, lower left on the map. They are seen in 1962, curving away from the trackbed of the line that continued in the distance and passed over the canal on a swing bridge. This link with the GWR was closed on 26th May 1938. The sidings were removed in 1969. (M.A.N.Johnston)

18.   The gasworks (lower left corner of the map) was dependent on the canal for coal transport until 1913, when a siding was provided. This view towards the works is from 1962; traffic ceased on 14th January 1971. All coal came by rail after 1913, a figure of 34,815 tons being recorded in 1938. Tar and oil were despatched by barge. (M.A.N.Johnston)

TUFFLEY JUNCTION

19.   We look at the area at the lower right corner of map IV, first with two northward views from Stroud Road bridge and then with two looking south from it. The postcard notes stated "MR and GWR Birmingham to Bristol trains meet near Gloucester. No. 751 and *Melbourne*". (P.Q.Treloar coll.)

20.   A view from 16th September 1975 features a special working. At that time, most trains used the Eastgate lines on the left, but these were closed on 1st December of that year. The four tracks southwards had become two on 18th August 1968. (T.Heavyside)

21.   The New Docks Branch curves right just before the signal box, which dates from 1979. It had 50 levers and was in use until 12th August 1968. No. 5936 *Oakley Hall* is working a local service on 13th July 1964. An up loop and four sidings were added for wartime traffic in 1941. (M.A.N.Johnston)

22.   A June 1975 panorama has the trackbed of the New Docks line, closed in 1971, under the car and the 1941 loop nearby. It was termed "Up and Down Depot Line" as it served the massive Quedgeley Depot. This was involved with munitions in both world wars and subsequently. It had about three miles of sidings, which were operated by the RAF latterly. The bridge carries the A38. (W.Potter/Kidderminster Railway Museum)

HARESFIELD

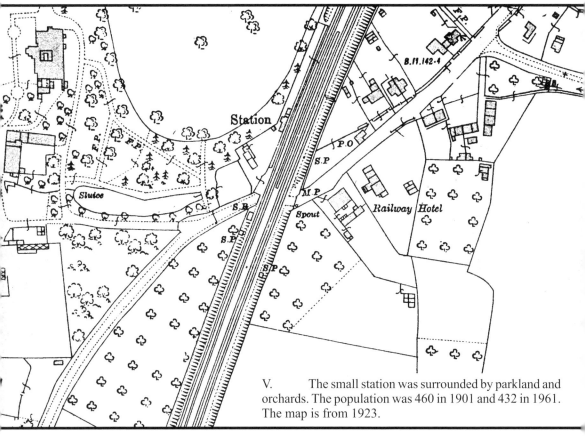

V.   The small station was surrounded by parkland and orchards. The population was 460 in 1901 and 432 in 1961. The map is from 1923.

23. The station was opened on 29th May 1854 by the MR. Platforms were never provided on the GWR lines. This is the up side in about 1900; the down platform was narrow and devoid of a shelter. (C.Maggs coll.)

24. A view across the level crossing from the signal box on 8th January 1961 includes 4-6-0 no. 45088 with a southbound express. The down platform timber structure remained until the station closed on 4th January 1965. The 16-lever box was reduced to a ground frame to control the gates from 15th September 1968. The same applied to the 25-lever Naas Crossing box, nearly two miles to the north. (M.A.N.Johnston)

MIDLAND RAILWAY. This Ticket is issued subject to the Regulations & Conditions stated in the Company's Time Tables & Bills.
FIRST ___ CLASS.
Gloucester to
SPEECH HOUSE ROAD
Via Sharpness
Gloucester S'Housell'd   Gloucester-S'Housell'd

MIDLAND RAILWAY This Ticket is issued subject to the Regulations & Conditions stated in the Company's Time Tables & Bills.
THIRD CLASS.   THIRD CLASS.
AVAILABLE ON DAY OF ISSUE ONLY.
GLOUCESTER to
HARESFIELD
FARE &   FARE 8d.
Gloucester-Haresfield   Gloucester-Haresfield

STANDISH JUNCTION

25.   The MR had to pay rent to the GWR for 20 years, until 1864, for the route north of the junction, although it had its own tracks from 22nd May 1854. We look south on 2nd October 1960, as a ballast train stands by the ex-MR 44-lever signal box. The tracks diverge beyond the curve, left to Swindon and straight on for Bristol. There were crossovers in the other direction behind the camera. (H.C.Casserley)

26.   A view in the opposite direction, but further north, on 4th August 1991 reveals the simplified layout. The HST forms the 12.15 Newcastle to Plymouth; the London lines are on the right. (M.Turvey)

STONEHOUSE
(BRISTOL ROAD)

S.P.

S.P.

F.B

S.B

Stonehouse Junction

S.P.

S.B

S.Ps

Goods Shed

Cattle Pens   W.M

VI.   The station opened with the line and the buildings were the most northerly of the BGR. The 1923 edition shows that there were no dwellings nearby. The GWR station was well situated in relation to the village, the population of which rose from 2183 in 1901 to 5311 in 1961. The turntable was removed in 1934. The suffix "Bristol Road" was added in 1951; Bradshaw used "Eastington Road" previously. Only the station house remained in 2004.

F.B   P

Station

Station

S.P.

Spring

NAILSWORTH M.R. BRANCH

F.P.

S.Ps

27.   A view north in 1923 includes both the goods shed and the signal box. A spare coach for branch line use is also evident. There was a siding for wool traffic behind the camera for many years. It was on the down side. There was a staff of 12 at about this time. (Stations UK)

28.   This southward panorama of chimneys from 1932 fails to reveal that the line passes over the A4096, the Stroudwater Canal, the River Frome and a mill stream, on a viaduct 90yds long. The sign refers to the covered way to the branch platform shown on the map. The suffix "Bristol Road" was added on 17th September 1951. (LGRP/NRM)

29.   The separate branch station was photographed in 1946. It was not used after June 1947. No. 1303 was an 0-4-4T of a type introduced by the MR in 1881. On the left is an MR spring point indicator. The lever could be used with pedal assistance. (LGRP/NRM)

30.   A 4F 0-6-0 is departing for Gloucester in this 1959 photograph, while 3F no. 43645 waits with freight from Nailsworth. The siding on the right served Hoffman's ball bearing works from 1940 to 1967. Passenger service was withdrawn on 4th January 1965 and freight followed on 1st June 1966. The 1897 signal box closed on 14th October 1968. The loop on the left was used as a coal concentration depot from 1966 until 1989 and 0-4-0 Drewry *Douglas* shunted there for many years. (M.A.N.Johnston)

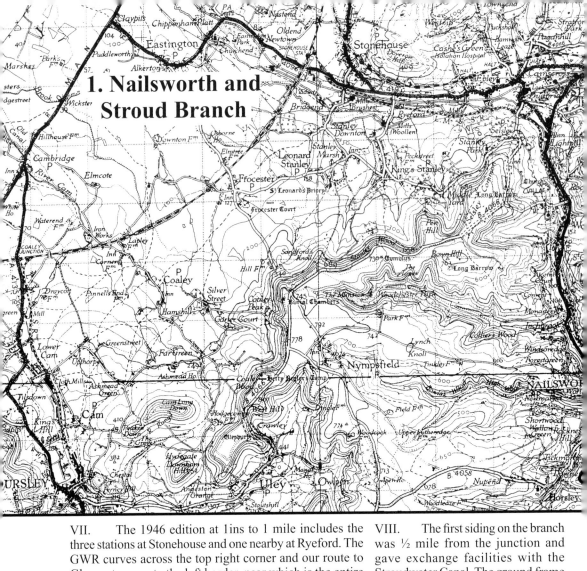

1. Nailsworth and Stroud Branch

VII.   The 1946 edition at 1ins to 1 mile includes the three stations at Stonehouse and one nearby at Ryeford. The GWR curves across the top right corner and our route to Gloucester runs to the left border, near which is the entire branch to Dursley. The location of Frocester station is also shown.

VIII.   The first siding on the branch was ½ mile from the junction and gave exchange facilities with the Stroudwater Canal. The ground frame was removed in 1958; there was a level crossing close to it.

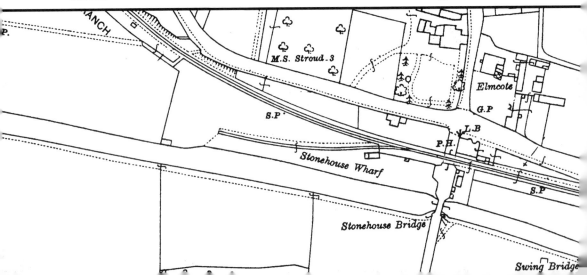

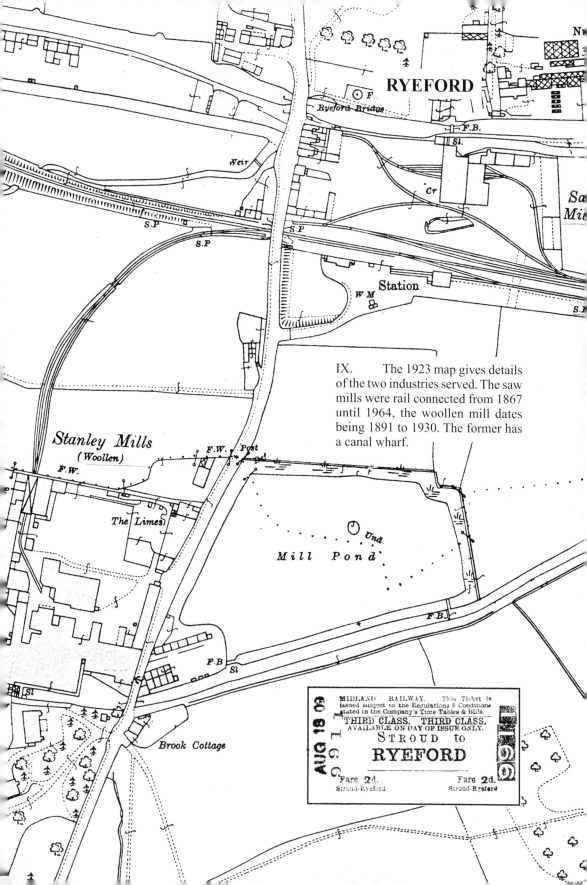

RYEFORD

Ryeford Bridge

Weir

Station

IX.   The 1923 map gives details of the two industries served. The saw mills were rail connected from 1867 until 1964, the woollen mill dates being 1891 to 1930. The former has a canal wharf.

Stanley Mills
(Woollen)

F.W.

The Limes

Mill Pond

Und.

Brook Cottage

MIDLAND RAILWAY. This Ticket is issued subject to the Regulations & Conditions stated in the Company's Time Tables & Bills.
THIRD CLASS.   THIRD CLASS.
AVAILABLE ON DAY OF ISSUE ONLY.
STROUD to RYEFORD
Fare 2d.   Fare 2d.
Stroud-Ryeford   Stroud-Ryeford

AUG 18 91

31. The station had an unusually wide platform, this last bearing passengers in 1947. The goods shed is included; service was withdrawn on 1st June 1966. The photo is from 1923. (Stations UK)

X. The 1936 survey is included to show the revised layout in the wood yard. It also shows the east end of the loop, plus the signal box, which closed on 7th September 1958.

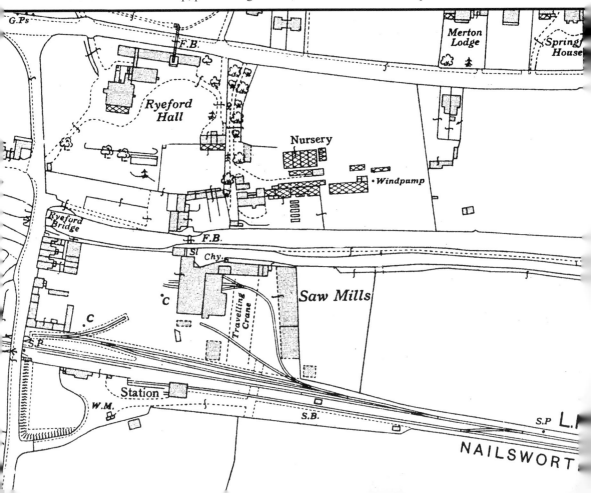

32.　　　Returning from Nailsworth in May 1947 is 0-4-4T no. 1330. Beyond the goods shed was a fertiliser store in the 1950s. There was a siding in the distance from 1873 to 1942, serving a mill on the north side of the line. It was initially used by William Lane who produced meal. On the right is the weigh house. (R.J.Buckley/SLS coll.)

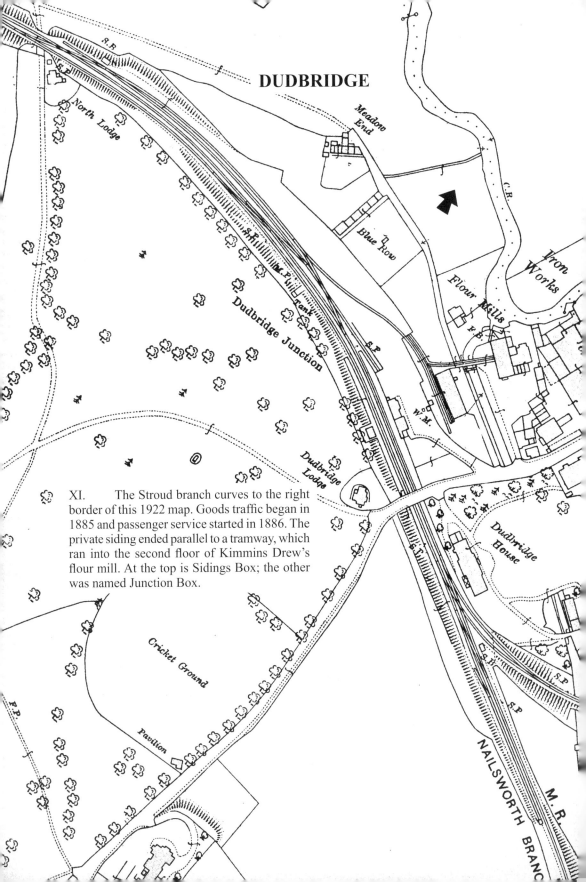

DUDBRIDGE

North Lodge

S.B.

Meadow End

Blue Row

C.R.

Iron Works

Flour Mills

F.B.

M.P.

Tank

S.P.

Dudbridge Junction

W.M.

Dudbridge Lodge

XI.   The Stroud branch curves to the right border of this 1922 map. Goods traffic began in 1885 and passenger service started in 1886. The private siding ended parallel to a tramway, which ran into the second floor of Kimmins Drew's flour mill. At the top is Sidings Box; the other was named Junction Box.

Dudbridge House

Cricket Ground

Pavilion

F.P.

S.P.

S.B.

S.P.

NAILSWORTH BRANCH

M.R.

33.   A train stands at the up platform, which was added in about July 1885, when the only loop on the branch came into use. A train for Stroud is signalled in this 1923 photograph. (Stations UK)

34.   This eastward view from 1958 shows how the up platform had been cut into the hillside and also includes the parcels shed. The yard had no goods shed or crane. The junction for Stroud is beyond the bridge. (R.M.Casserley)

35.   The north elevation was recorded in 1958, more than ten years after the last passenger had passed through the door behind the Hillman. Beyond the Austin are stored coaches. The fine structure was demolished in the 1970s. (H.C.Casserley)

36.   The signal box was in use from 15th January 1924 until 7th December 1957, when the passing loop was removed. It served as a ground frame at that time and was demolished in 1966. A 3F 0-6-0 is arriving from Stroud in 1958. (M.A.N.Johnston)

XII.   This 1922 extract has the line from Dudbridge top left, in a cutting. Trains emerged from it onto a 145yd-long curved viaduct, before entering the station. There were two ground frames, but no signal box. The crane was of 5-ton capacity and is at the east end of the yard. The suffix "Cheapside" was applied by Bradshaw for many years; "Wallbridge" was also used by some. Inset is the gasworks siding, which was west of the viaduct. Coal came to the 1833 works by canal until about 1921, when a bridge was built over the River Frome to carry a two-foot gauge railway for conveyance of coal from the MR. Around 25,000 tons were consumed annually prior to closure in 1958.

37.　　Few passengers were recorded here, as most towns were more conveniently reached by the GWR. The station was noted for its floral displays and is seen in September 1910. The timber structure outlasted the railway, being used for commercial purposes subsequently. (L.Padin coll.)

38.　　This view towards the goods yard was recorded in 1947, shortly before withdrawal of passenger services and when there was a full complement of gas lamps, plus one seat. There were no doors on the approach road side. (LGRP/NRM)

39.	An eastward panorama from 1959 includes 3F 0-6-0 no. 43754, the canopies of the goods shed and a bridge on the Swindon line in the background. There had been a siding for Wood & Rowes to the left of the loco until about 1936. (M.A.N.Johnston)

40.	BR class 2 2-6-0 no. 78001 is in the dock siding on 24th April 1964. The cattle pens were adjacent to this line. The track diverging in the foreground ran through the long goods shed. (M.A.N.Johnston)

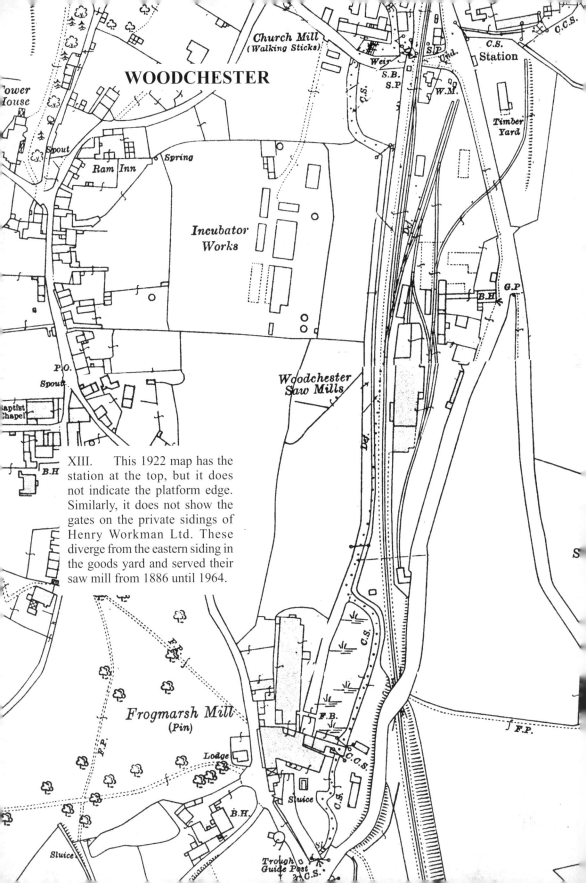

WOODCHESTER

Church Mill
(Walking Sticks)

Weir

C.S. Station

Timber Yard

ower House

Spout

Ram Inn

Spring

Incubator Works

B.H

G.P

P.O.

Spout

Woodchester Saw Mills

aptist Chapel

B.H

XIII. This 1922 map has the station at the top, but it does not indicate the platform edge. Similarly, it does not show the gates on the private sidings of Henry Workman Ltd. These diverge from the eastern siding in the goods yard and served their saw mill from 1886 until 1964.

Frogmarsh Mill
(Pin)

Lodge

F.B.

C.S.

F.P.

Sluice

B.H.

Sluice

Trough
Guide Post
C.S.

41.   Unlike the other stations on the route and although it opened with the branch, a cheap wooden structure was provided here. Only the gentleman's toilet and the chimneys were of brick construction. Wiring was in progress when this photo was taken in 1923. The number of residents changed little: 820 in 1901 and 815 in 1961. (Stations UK)

42.   A 1958 southward view includes a full set of lamps, the station house, the goods shed beyond it and the crossing keepers hut. The gas pipe runs below the platform edge. (R.M.Casserley)

43.	We end our survey with two photos from 1959. This shows that the fireman had to open the crossing gates by that time. The guard usually closed them. Some MR diagonal fencing is evident. (M.A.N.Johnston)

44.	The goods yard was theoretically open until branch closure in 1966, but there is no evidence of traffic. At least the regulation fire buckets were still in place. (M.A.N.Johnston)

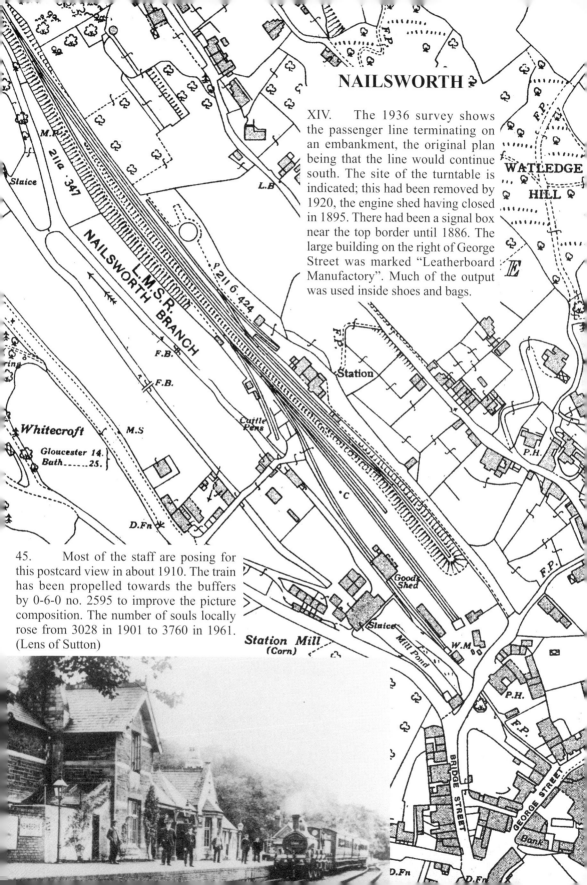

NAILSWORTH

XIV. The 1936 survey shows the passenger line terminating on an embankment, the original plan being that the line would continue south. The site of the turntable is indicated; this had been removed by 1920, the engine shed having closed in 1895. There had been a signal box near the top border until 1886. The large building on the right of George Street was marked "Leatherboard Manufactory". Much of the output was used inside shoes and bags.

45. Most of the staff are posing for this postcard view in about 1910. The train has been propelled towards the buffers by 0-6-0 no. 2595 to improve the picture composition. The number of souls locally rose from 3028 in 1901 to 3760 in 1961. (Lens of Sutton)

46.   This photo from 1936 indicates the great height difference between the two parts of the station. The end of the platform is upper right and part of the goods yard is in the foreground. The branch from Stonehouse was converted to a cycle path in 1984. (SLS coll.)

47.   The architecture was certainly designed to impress, with tapered chimneys, ornamental gables and a bold bay window. The photograph is from 1947. (LGRP/NRM)

48.   Details worthy of study include the perforated barge boards, the complex porch gable and, most importantly, the fine stone turned columns of the portico, which had intricate carved capitals. The photo is from 1956. (R.M.Casserley)

49.   Shunting the yard on 4th April 1961 was MR-built class 4 0-6-0 no. 43924, which is now resident on the Keighley & Worth Valley Railway. The platform lines were lifted in 1964. Further north, there had been Dunkirk siding (until 1947) and one for United Brassfounders (until 1918). The crane was rated at five tons. (M.A.N.Johnston)

FROCESTER

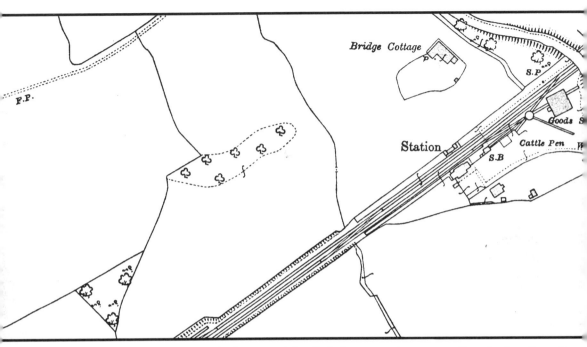

XV.   Returning to the main line, we visit a little known and remote station, the location of which is to be seen near the centre of map VII. This extract here is from 1922. The up refuge siding (lower left) was in use from 1920 to 1924.

50.   This postcard view is from about 1910 and includes the 1899 signal box. Beyond the bridge, there was a siding on the left to a gravel pit from 1917 to 1924. There was a population of 239 in 1901. (Lens of Sutton)

51. Few wagon turntables remained in use in 1961 when this photo was taken. The canopies had long gone, as had most passengers. Service was withdrawn on 11th December of that year; so were goods facilities. (D.Ibbotson/R.S.Carpenter)

52. "The Devonian" was recorded racing through on 23rd March 1963, bound for Paignton. The signal box remained in use until 11th May 1966. The population had dropped to 206 by 1961. (M.A.N.Johnston)

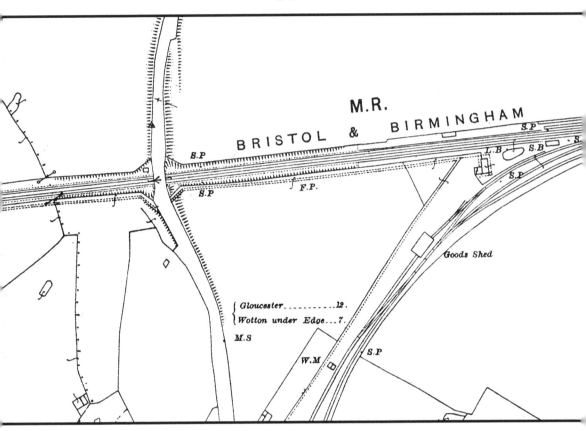

53.　　We can now enjoy three photographs from 1956. No. 45607 *Fiji* arrives with the 9.10am stopping train from Bristol on 3rd March. There was no footbridge. (R.M.Casserley)

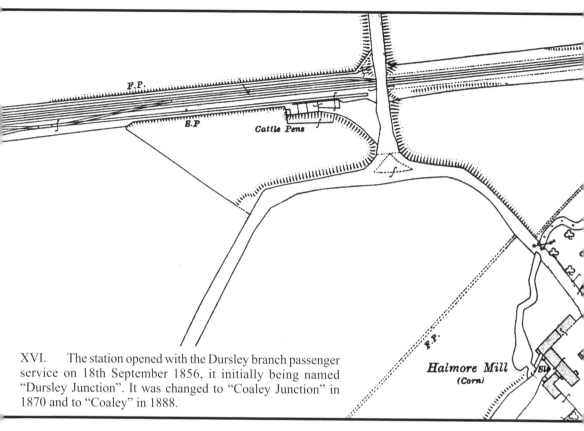

XVI.   The station opened with the Dursley branch passenger service on 18th September 1856, it initially being named "Dursley Junction". It was changed to "Coaley Junction" in 1870 and to "Coaley" in 1888.

F.P.

S.P

Cattle Pens

Halmore Mill
(Corn)

F.P.

54.   The trailing connection in the foreground was supplemented by a facing one in 1890. Standing in the branch platform is an example of a typical mixed train. (H.C.Casserley)

55.　　The flat-roofed extension on the left was added by BR; the other part was earlier and included the gents. A Ford 8 stands near no. 41720, which is about to leave for Dursley at 4.30pm on 28th April. A contemporary photographer noted that travelling on this train was Cam Camwell as it ran alongside the River Cam to enter Cam station. Cam had 1717 residents in 1901. (W.A.Camwell/SLS)

56.　　Construction was in red brick with limestone quoins. The offices were built by the D&MJR, whereas the goods shed was erected by the MR. This was still standing in 2004. An ancient barrow stands by a modern coach on 25th August 1958, while the postman leaves his van and we enjoy the garden. The hut on the left was for lamps. (A.E.Bennett)

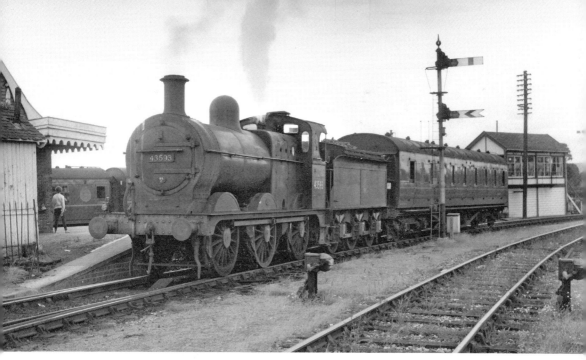

57. The LMS replaced the MR signal box in 1935 with the one seen. No. 43593 blows off on 10th September 1962 before beginning its gentle excursion up the valley to Dursley on the last day of passenger operation. (G.Adams/M.J.Stretton coll.)

CAM & DURSLEY

58. The station was opened on 29th May 1994, near the site of the cattle pens. No. 150221 was working the 13.28 Gloucester to Weston-super-Mare service on 27th October 1994. (C.G.Maggs)

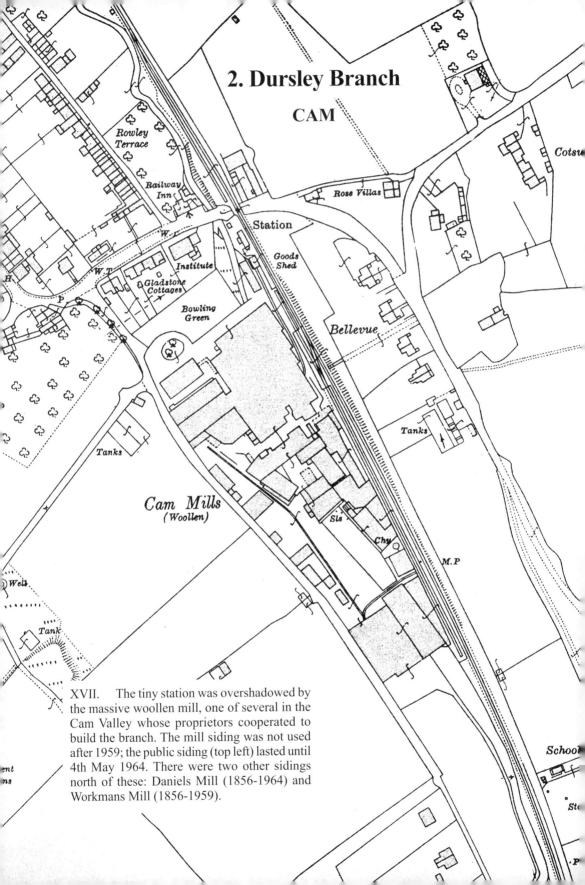

2. Dursley Branch
CAM

Rowley Terrace

Railway Inn

Rose Villas

Cotsw

Station

W.

Goods Shed

Institute

W.T.

Gladstone Cottages

Bowling Green

Bellevue

Tanks

Tanks

Cam Mills
(Woollen)

Sls

Chy

M.P

Well

Tank

School

St

XVII.   The tiny station was overshadowed by the massive woollen mill, one of several in the Cam Valley whose proprietors cooperated to build the branch. The mill siding was not used after 1959; the public siding (top left) lasted until 4th May 1964. There were two other sidings north of these: Daniels Mill (1856-1964) and Workmans Mill (1856-1959).

59.   Although small, the building was finely detailed with good craftsmanship evident in the stonework of the doorway and in the bargeboards. The goods shed contrasted in its simplicity. A short tramway ran from the back of it into the mill. The photo is from 1932. (LGRP/NRM)

60.   There was a station master and two porters in the 1920s. The branch was operated as "One Engine in Steam", thus the signals served only to protect the crossing. The goods siding is beyond the gates in this 1959 view. Distant signals were also provided; one of their wires is on the right. (H.C.Casserley)

61.   The 4.15pm from Dursley was hauled by 0-6-0PT no. 6415 on 18th June 1960. There is evidence of recent coal traffic in the yard. Prior to World War II, Hunt & Winterbotham had their own coal wagons to bring supplies to their mill, the chimneys of which can be seen in the background. (P.J.Kelley)

SOUTH OF CAM

62.   The D&MJR ceased to operate its line in 1861 and sold it to the MR. The early history is vague, but the MR provided trains from 1857 on lease. Their engine shed was subsequently occupied by a locomotive sent out from Gloucester each week. Dursley is in the distance in this 1951 picture. The shed was closed on 10th September 1962, when passenger service ceased. (H.C.Casserley)

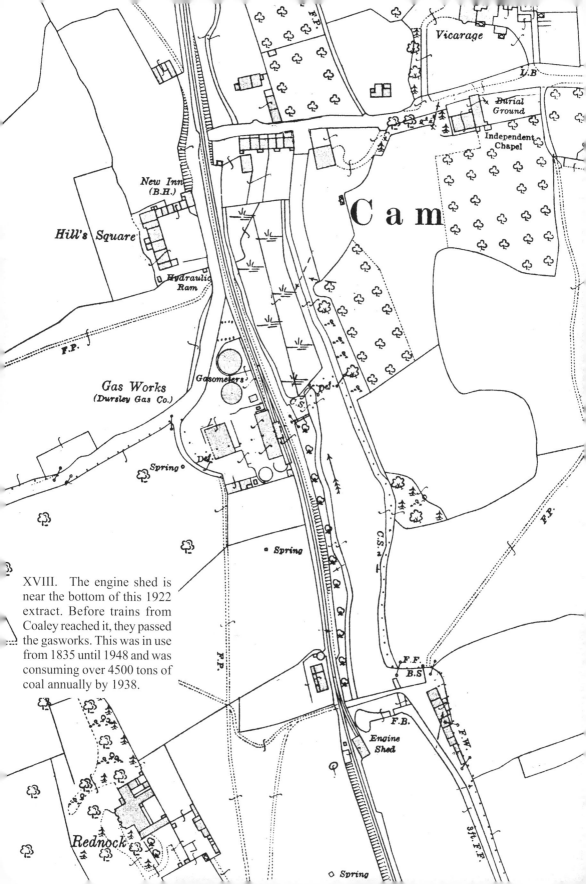

XVIII. The engine shed is near the bottom of this 1922 extract. Before trains from Coaley reached it, they passed the gasworks. This was in use from 1835 until 1948 and was consuming over 4500 tons of coal annually by 1938.

DURSLEY

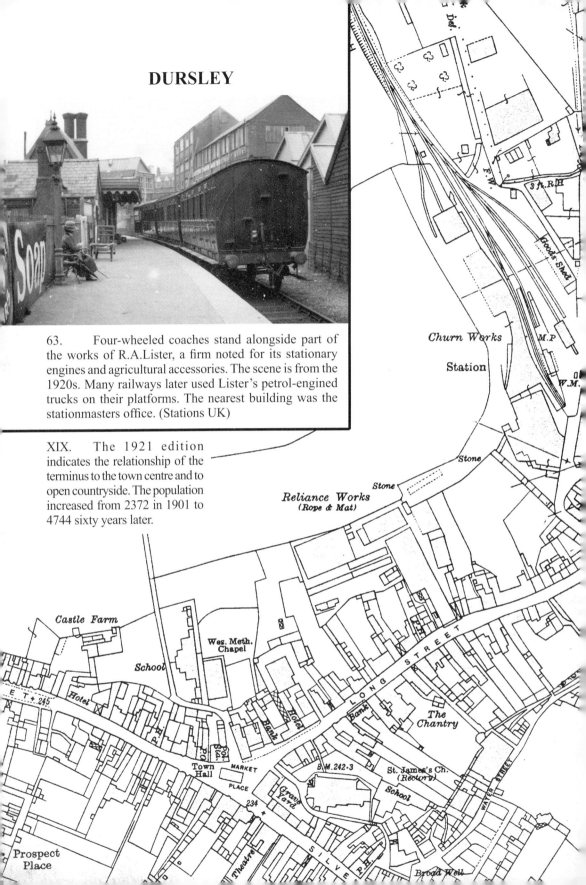

63.　　Four-wheeled coaches stand alongside part of the works of R.A.Lister, a firm noted for its stationary engines and agricultural accessories. The scene is from the 1920s. Many railways later used Lister's petrol-engined trucks on their platforms. The nearest building was the stationmasters office. (Stations UK)

XIX.　　The 1921 edition indicates the relationship of the terminus to the town centre and to open countryside. The population increased from 2372 in 1901 to 4744 sixty years later.

64.   No. 1720 approaches the platform on 5th July 1947. The run-round loop is behind it. Listers had private sidings on both sides of the often-busy goods yard. (H.C.Casserley)

65.   A 1952 record reveals the inevitable wartime neglect which was slow to be rectified, particularly in such rural outposts. (LGRP/NRM)

66.   A 1956 southward panorama has the platform in the distance and Lister's 1918 siding to the right of no. 41748. Another was added to the left of the camera in 1930 and extended later. Listers had another siding beyond the gasworks in 1905-09. (H.C.Casserley)

67.   A January 1961 record reveals that, when the building was eventually renovated, most of the canopy was removed. The goods sheds are evident, as is more of Lister's premises. Public goods traffic ceased on 28th June 1968, but the 2½ mile long branch remained as a private siding for Listers until July 1970. Their works then spread across the site and the station was demolished. (E.Wilmshurst)

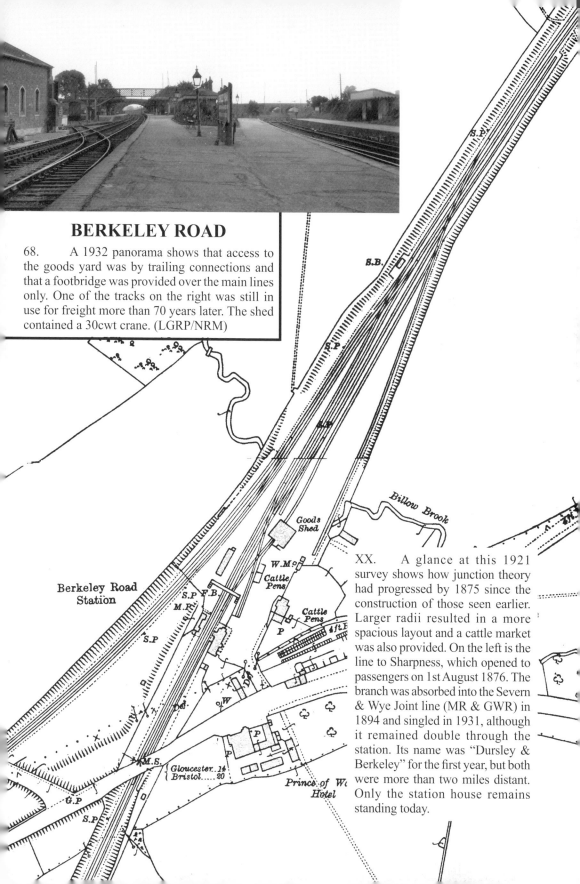

BERKELEY ROAD

68.　　A 1932 panorama shows that access to the goods yard was by trailing connections and that a footbridge was provided over the main lines only. One of the tracks on the right was still in use for freight more than 70 years later. The shed contained a 30cwt crane. (LGRP/NRM)

XX.　　A glance at this 1921 survey shows how junction theory had progressed by 1875 since the construction of those seen earlier. Larger radii resulted in a more spacious layout and a cattle market was also provided. On the left is the line to Sharpness, which opened to passengers on 1st August 1876. The branch was absorbed into the Severn & Wye Joint line (MR & GWR) in 1894 and singled in 1931, although it remained double through the station. Its name was "Dursley & Berkeley" for the first year, but both were more than two miles distant. Only the station house remains standing today.

69.   A closer view of the buildings has the 1875 one near the garden and the 1844 structure in the background. No. 1064 is heading the 5.15pm Bristol to Gloucester local train on 5th July 1947. (H.C.Casserley)

70.   A train departs for Bristol on 9th July 1959. The station had lost its all-round canopy from Brunel's drawing board and the inside-keyed track that was present for many years. The site was levelled in about 1965. (H.C.Casserley)

71.		A footbridge panorama on 2nd October 1960 includes ex-GWR 0-4-2T no. 1420 with a Lydney train. This service was withdrawn on 26th of that month following the destruction of the Severn Bridge by an errant barge. A shuttle to Sharpness was maintained until 2nd November 1964, but freight continues. All passenger traffic here ceased on 4th January 1965. (H.C.Casserley)

72.		The goods shed and part of the flower bed were photographed in 1960. Freight traffic ended on 1st November 1966. There had been more sidings one mile to the north at Gossington, from 1916 to 1926. They served a munitions depot at Slimbridge. (R.S.Carpenter)

SOUTH OF BERKELEY ROAD

XXI. The station is top right and the line to Sharpness is on the left. As this 1927 map shows, the Berkeley Road Loop was GWR property. It was opened in 1908, purely as a diversionary route for use when the Severn Tunnel was closed. This use ceased when the bridge was severed in 1960 and the loop was subsequently little used, closing on 27th January 1963. South Junction signal box (20 levers) closed that day, but the box at the station (45 levers) lasted until 14th October 1968, when it was replaced by a ground frame. One mile beyond South Junction was Bendalls Siding of 1890. It served a mill and was used intermittently until about 1912. The scale is 6ins to 1 mile.

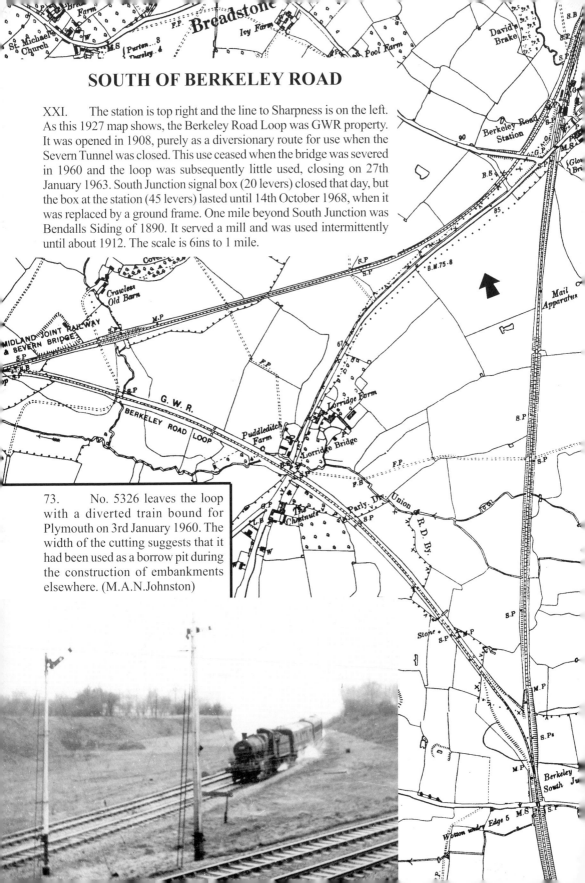

73. No. 5326 leaves the loop with a diverted train bound for Plymouth on 3rd January 1960. The width of the cutting suggests that it had been used as a borrow pit during the construction of embankments elsewhere. (M.A.N.Johnston)

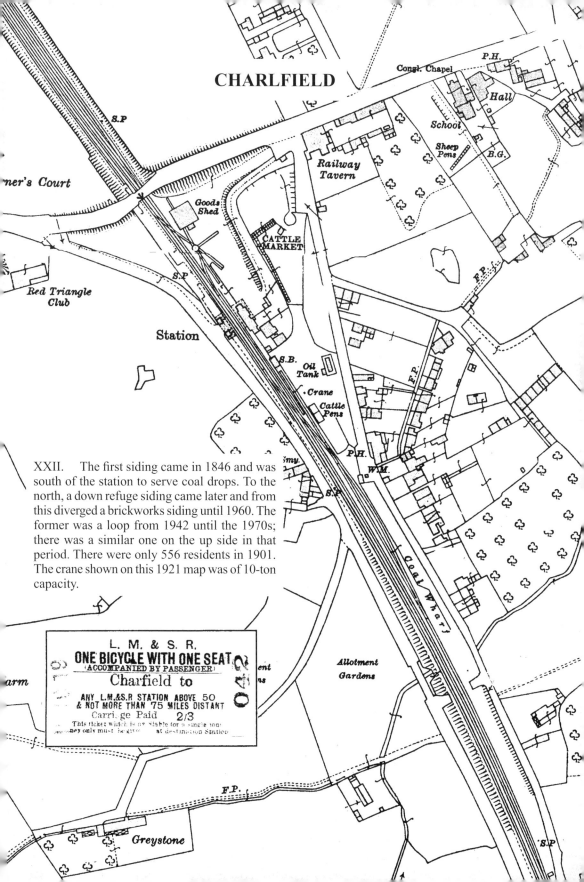

CHARLFIELD

Congl. Chapel · P.H.

Hall

School

Sheep Pens · B.G.

Railway Tavern

Goods Shed

CATTLE MARKET

F.P.

Red Triangle Club

S.P.

Station

S.B. · Oil Tank

Crane

Cattle Pens

F.P.

P.H.

W.M.

S.P.

Coal Wharf

XXII.   The first siding came in 1846 and was south of the station to serve coal drops. To the north, a down refuge siding came later and from this diverged a brickworks siding until 1960. The former was a loop from 1942 until the 1970s; there was a similar one on the up side in that period. There were only 556 residents in 1901. The crane shown on this 1921 map was of 10-ton capacity.

Allotment Gardens

L. M. & S. R.
ONE BICYCLE WITH ONE SEAT
(ACCOMPANIED BY PASSENGER)
Charfield to
ANY L.M.&S.R STATION ABOVE 50
& NOT MORE THAN 75 MILES DISTANT
Carriage Paid   2/3
This ticket which is available for a single journey only must be given up at destination Station

Greystone

F.P.

S.P.

74.   A 1933 southward panorama includes the goods shed (which housed a 30cwt crane), the turntable (which was removed in December 1956), the 1847 station house (beyond which projects a large water tank), Brunel's station building (with complete canopies) and beyond is the 29-lever signal box of 1909, which closed on 16th May 1971. (LGRP/NRM)

75.   From the same viewpoint on 5th May 1982, we see a class 45 with the 15.05 Plymouth to Manchester service. Local passenger trains ceased on 4th January 1965 and goods services ended on 5th September following. There is a ground frame near the third coach for the crossovers. The loops were still in place in 2004, as were the buildings. (T.Heavyside)

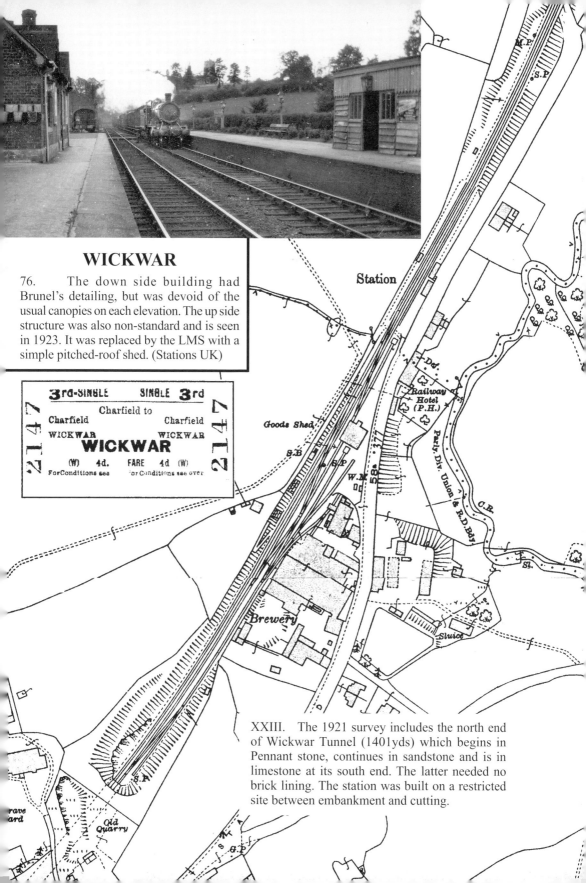

WICKWAR

76.   The down side building had Brunel's detailing, but was devoid of the usual canopies on each elevation. The up side structure was also non-standard and is seen in 1923. It was replaced by the LMS with a simple pitched-roof shed. (Stations UK)

Station

XXIII.   The 1921 survey includes the north end of Wickwar Tunnel (1401yds) which begins in Pennant stone, continues in sandstone and is in limestone at its south end. The latter needed no brick lining. The station was built on a restricted site between embankment and cutting.

77.　　This view is from the end of the up platform in 1959 and includes part of the brewery, which also produced cider. It had its own siding from 1860 until 1954. The signal box was in use from 1908 to 2nd November 1965; the goods yard closed on 10th June 1963. The box was rescued and moved to a site east of the line. (D.Ibbotson/R.S.Carpenter coll.)

78.　　Constructed on steeply sloping land, the road side of the buildings had two storeys, with a flight of steps to the platforms between the structures. There was a population of 405 in 1901, this rising to only 888 by 1961. Trains ceased to call on 4th January 1965. (D.Ibbotson/R.S.Carpenter coll.)

SOUTH OF WICKWAR

79.   Smoke belches from the mouth of Wickwar Tunnel, as no. 5552 Silver Jubilee tears south in May 1935. An iron trough had to be provided to carry a stream over the line and it was boarded over to create a safe and convenient crossing for a footpath. (LGRP/NRM)

80.   Seen at the same location on 5th May 1982 is the 09.50 Edinburgh to Plymouth HST. Unusually, this tunnel mouth had no portal and was simply raw limestone, like this end of the tunnel. The entrance now has a brick lining. The train would soon pass the sites of Rangeworthy signal box (10 levers. 1942-69) and the sidings of three collieries, which had been on the west side of the line between 1883 and 1906. (T.Heavyside)

XXIV. The Thornbury branch curves to the left of this 1921 map, while the main line at the bottom continues on the next map into Yate station. Two signal boxes are shown; the one on the branch closed on 14th November 1926, the other on 20th October 1969, after which date it was used as a ground frame. There had been a turntable in the vee of the junction until about 1900.

Stover

Stover Farm

Varren Farm

Yate Junction

Cattle Pens

F.B.

S.P.

S.P.

S.B.

S.P.

P

S.P.

S.P.

W.M.

S.P.

W

M.P.

S.B.

F.P.

81.   On the left is the Thornbury branch, which carried passengers from 1872 until 1944. General goods ceased on 3rd September 1967, but the branch reopened for stone traffic on 3rd July 1972. Sidings in the distance on the down side served an aircraft factory from 1918 to 1954. Yate Main Line Junction box had 40 levers. (M.A.N.Johnston)

82.   An HST screams south on 20th March 1999 and passes the short length of double track on the branch. They converge before joining the up line, this being signalled for reversible running southwards to Westerleigh Junction since 1972. (M.Turvey)

Allotment Gardens

YATE

National
Concrete Slab Factory

G.P

233

Yate
Station

Goods
Shed

F.B.

XXV.   This map continues from the previous one and includes Yate South Junction box. Here the GWR lines join the LMS main line, one each side of it. They were mainly used for trains diverted onto the Severn Bridge. The box was open from 1897 to 1903 in connection with the construction of the GWR's Badminton line. It reopened on 1st March 1908 and its 20-lever frame was in use until 10th May 1971. The main line southwards was closed to passenger services on 3rd January 1970 and all such trains ran via Westerleigh Junction and the route west thereof (see next map). Yate housed 1279 souls in 1901, 3878 in 1961 and 20,640 in 2001. The station house survived in 2004.

S.P.

S.B.

S.P.

M.P.

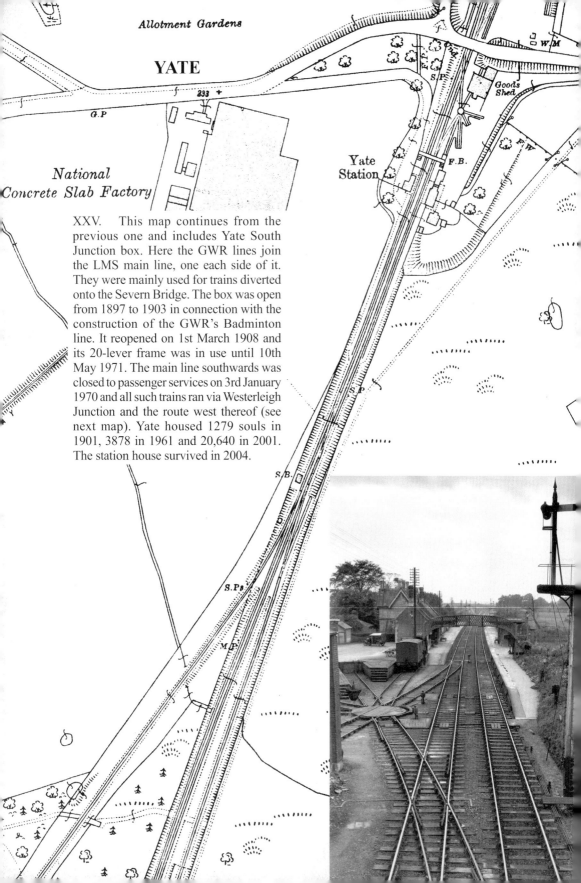

(lower left) 83. A 1935 southward view includes the now familiar track layout, which was supplemented by the sidings seen in picture 81. The turntable lasted until about 1955 and all local freight ceased on 20th June 1966. (LGRP/NRM)

84.　　Looking north in September 1960, we see the BGR buildings of Brunel's design and the slightly later station house. Passenger service was withdrawn on 4th January 1965. (R.M.Casserley)

85.　　New platforms were opened on 11th May 1989 and they were later lengthened to take four coaches instead of two. A basic service of six trains was provided, weekdays only, and 65 car park spaces were created. No. 150251 is departing for Gloucester on 20th March 1999. (M.Turvey)

3. Thornbury Branch

XXVI. This extract at 1ins to 1 mile includes the entire length of the 1872 branch, together with the colliery branch west of Westerleigh. This and Westerleigh Junction are considered after we have enjoyed a trip to Thornbury.

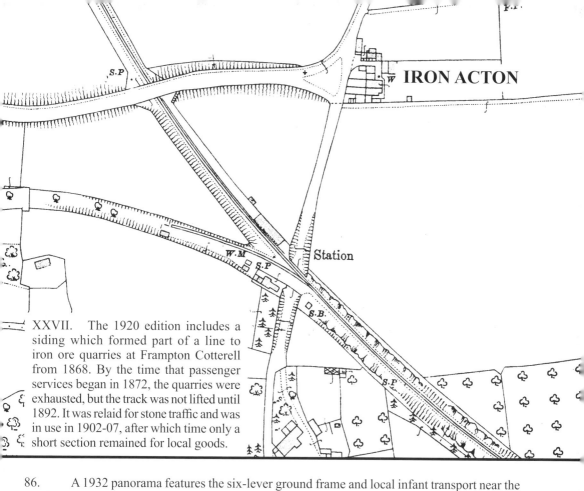

IRON ACTON

XXVII. The 1920 edition includes a siding which formed part of a line to iron ore quarries at Frampton Cotterell from 1868. By the time that passenger services began in 1872, the quarries were exhausted, but the track was not lifted until 1892. It was relaid for stone traffic and was in use in 1902-07, after which time only a short section remained for local goods.

Station

86.   A 1932 panorama features the six-lever ground frame and local infant transport near the catch point. There had been a small signal box behind the camera until 1928. (LGRP/NRM)

87.   An enthusiasts special railtour is seen from the bridge northwest of the station on 15th April 1956. It was named "Severn Venturer" and started from Swindon, crossed the Severn Bridge and toured the Forest of Dean. (Stations UK)

88.   A 1960 record includes the station house and a coal wagon nearby. Only a shed and clothes line then occupied the platform. An Automatic Open Crossing is now provided for stone trains and a new crossing on the new B4508, beyond the bridge, is train crew operated. The gate on the far left doubled as a goods yard gate. (M.A.N.Johnston)

TYTHERINGTON

89.   We are looking down the 1 in 61 gradient towards Iron Acton on 2nd July 1960, from the bridge over Station Road. The map is overleaf. (M.A.N.Johnston)

90.   A view from the platform on the same day includes the West Quarry connection, which was in use from 1895 to 1963. In the distance is the site of Church Quarry siding, which carried stone from 1898 to about 1944. Beyond it is the 224yd long Tytherington Tunnel and beyond that were Grovesend Quarry sidings from 1888 to 1967. (M.A.N.Johnston)

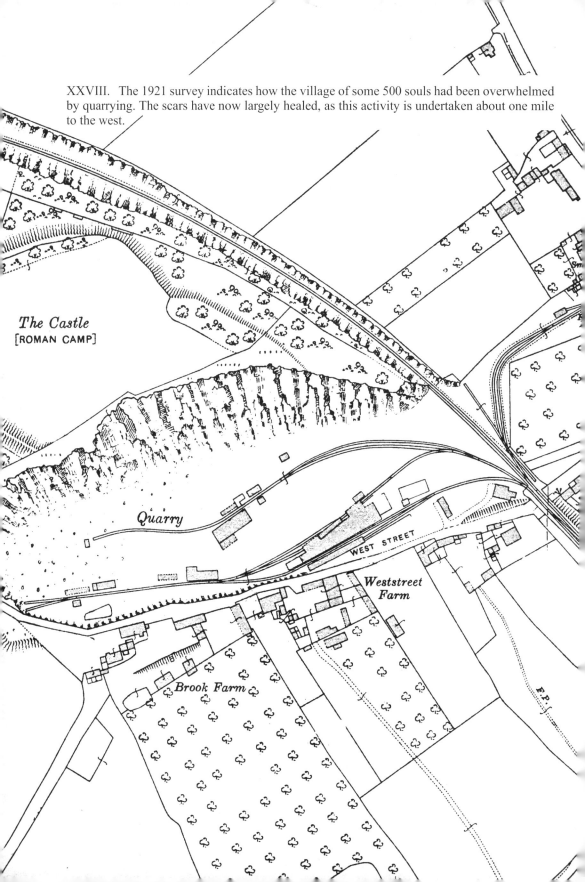

XXVIII. The 1921 survey indicates how the village of some 500 souls had been overwhelmed by quarrying. The scars have now largely healed, as this activity is undertaken about one mile to the west.

The Castle
[ROMAN CAMP]

Quarry

WEST STREET

Weststreet Farm

Brook Farm

F.P.

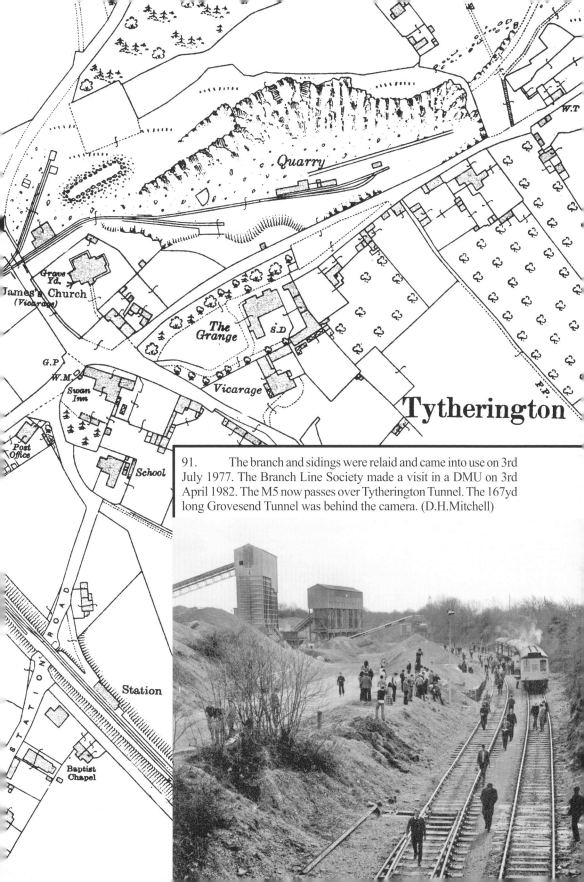

Tytherington

91.   The branch and sidings were relaid and came into use on 3rd July 1977. The Branch Line Society made a visit in a DMU on 3rd April 1982. The M5 now passes over Tytherington Tunnel. The 167yd long Grovesend Tunnel was behind the camera. (D.H.Mitchell)

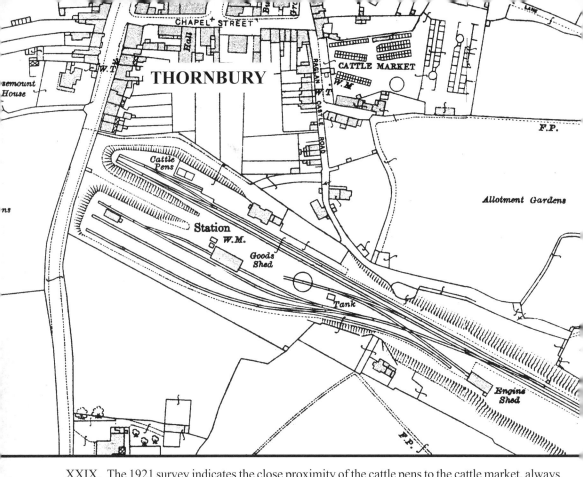

XXIX. The 1921 survey indicates the close proximity of the cattle pens to the cattle market, always important if passengers were to keep their shoes clean. The turntable was in use until 1957.

92.   No. 3419 was of a MR design dating back to 1885 and it is seen in LMS livery on 12th September 1936. For many years, passenger trains worked through to Bristol, providing a suburban service for the city. (SLS coll.)

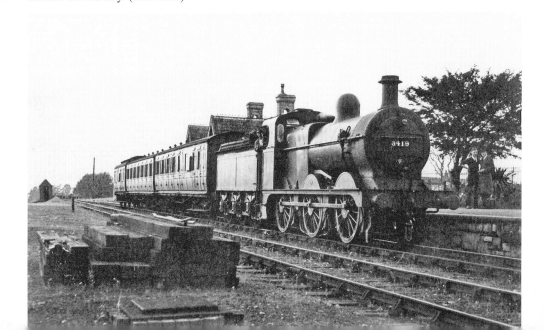

93.   The RCTS ran a railtour on 26th September 1959 using 0-6-0PT no. 9769 and it is seen from near the buffers of the cattle siding. Regular passenger trains had ceased in 1944, but freight continued until 1967. The goods shed had a 30cwt crane. (G.Adams/ M.J.Stretton coll.)

94.   A few minutes later, no. 9769 passes the engine shed, which had closed on 19th June 1944. There is a shelter for the ground frame; there had been a signal box until 1886. The line climbs at 1 in 61 for one mile. (G.Adams/ M.J.Stretton coll.)

95.   Fenestrated chimneys and carved barge boards were among the attractions of this rural gem, which had some of the best of MR architecture. The local population rose from 2594 in 1901 to 3473 in 1961, but most found the bus to Bristol preferable; it was certainly more direct and cheaper. (LGRP/NRM)

WESTERLEIGH

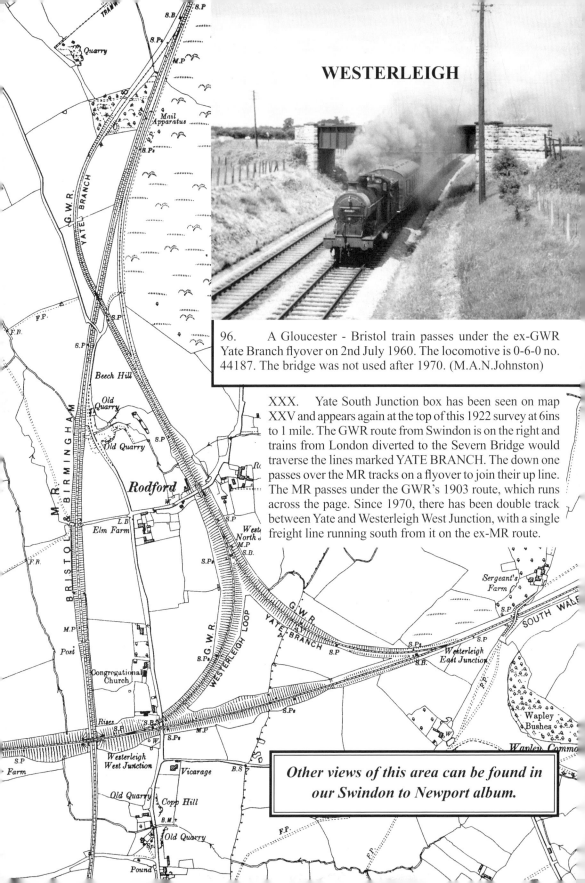

96.   A Gloucester - Bristol train passes under the ex-GWR Yate Branch flyover on 2nd July 1960. The locomotive is 0-6-0 no. 44187. The bridge was not used after 1970. (M.A.N.Johnston)

XXX.   Yate South Junction box has been seen on map XXV and appears again at the top of this 1922 survey at 6ins to 1 mile. The GWR route from Swindon is on the right and trains from London diverted to the Severn Bridge would traverse the lines marked YATE BRANCH. The down one passes over the MR tracks on a flyover to join their up line. The MR passes under the GWR's 1903 route, which runs across the page. Since 1970, there has been double track between Yate and Westerleigh West Junction, with a single freight line running south from it on the ex-MR route.

Other views of this area can be found in our Swindon to Newport album.

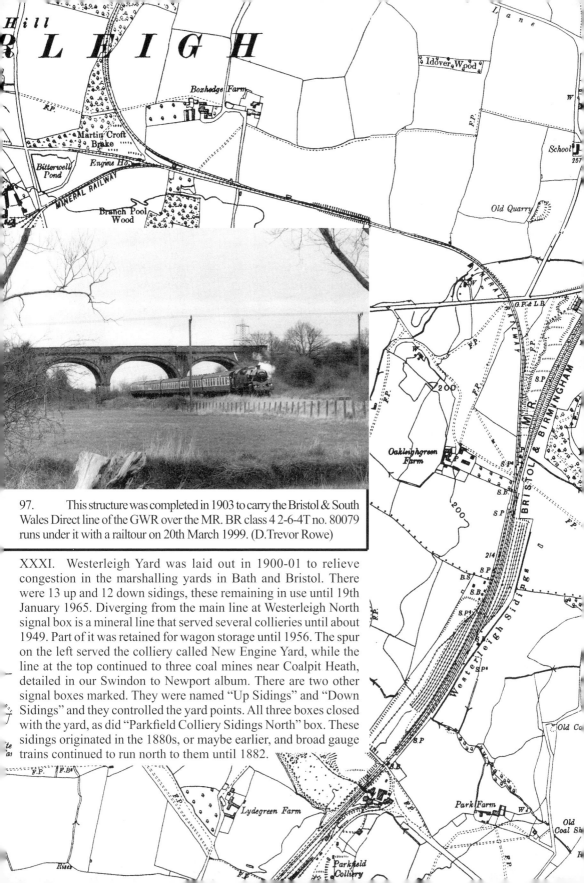

97.   This structure was completed in 1903 to carry the Bristol & South Wales Direct line of the GWR over the MR. BR class 4 2-6-4T no. 80079 runs under it with a railtour on 20th March 1999. (D.Trevor Rowe)

XXXI.   Westerleigh Yard was laid out in 1900-01 to relieve congestion in the marshalling yards in Bath and Bristol. There were 13 up and 12 down sidings, these remaining in use until 19th January 1965. Diverging from the main line at Westerleigh North signal box is a mineral line that served several collieries until about 1949. Part of it was retained for wagon storage until 1956. The spur on the left served the colliery called New Engine Yard, while the line at the top continued to three coal mines near Coalpit Heath, detailed in our Swindon to Newport album. There are two other signal boxes marked. They were named "Up Sidings" and "Down Sidings" and they controlled the yard points. All three boxes closed with the yard, as did "Parkfield Colliery Sidings North" box. These sidings originated in the 1880s, or maybe earlier, and broad gauge trains continued to run north to them until 1882.

98.　　Avon County Council opened a waste terminal in the vicinity of the Up Sidings box on 19th November 1985, rubbish going to Calvert, Bucks., until 30th March 2001, when the terminal closed. Murco Petroleum created an oil distribution depot nearby, operation commencing on 1st March 1991. As many as 32 tankers of 100 tonne capacity can be unloaded at once. The waste container loading gantry is in the background as no. 60015 *Bow Fell* returns empties to Robeston on 17th March 1997. (M.J.Stretton)

99.　　The southern limit of the single line is close to the M4 and here an engineers training school was established. Tamping instruction was given using the machines on the left of this picture from 24th March 2004. Featured is a "User-Worked Crossing". (C.Porter)

NORTH OF MANGOTSFIELD

XXXII. This map continues from the previous one and includes South Pit, which had sidings in use between 1861 and 1940. Shortwood Brickworks had sidings from 1865 until 1964. The final signal box functioned from November 1890 to 22nd February 1965. It had 12 levers. Lower left is Mangotsfield North Junction box, which was open from 1889 until 4th January 1970, when through running to Bristol ceased. It had a 25-lever frame. The first Mangotsfield station had been in this vicinity until 4th August 1869.

100.   Photographed against the light in 1932, this indifferent quality panorama includes (from left to right) the station approach, the original buildings, North Junction box, the line to Bath curving left (between the telephone pole and the signal post) and three carriage sidings. The siding in front of the building was used for local goods traffic until 10th June 1963. (Brunel University/Mowat coll.)

101.   A view in the opposite direction on 23rd January 1965 includes the siding seen left of centre in the previous picture, new junction signals and class 8F no. 48000, bound for Bristol. The route from here to the centre of the city can now be traversed on foot or cycle, thanks largely to Heritage Lottery Funding. (T.Nicholls)

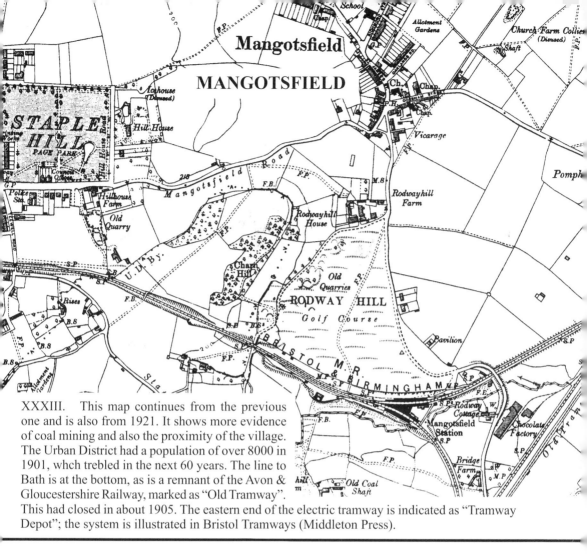

XXXIII. This map continues from the previous one and is also from 1921. It shows more evidence of coal mining and also the proximity of the village. The Urban District had a population of over 8000 in 1901, which trebled in the next 60 years. The line to Bath is at the bottom, as is a remnant of the Avon & Gloucestershire Railway, marked as "Old Tramway". This had closed in about 1905. The eastern end of the electric tramway is indicated as "Tramway Depot"; the system is illustrated in Bristol Tramways (Middleton Press).

102.   A 1923 panorama has a goods train arriving from Westerleigh Yard on the left and the Bath platforms on the right. Coaches stand in the down bay, which was used for some suburban services to Bristol. (Stations UK)

103.   Station Junction box is visible as 2-4-0 no. 155 stands at the head of a Bath-Bristol train on 29th May 1929. This 1876 locomotive ran until 1950; its potted history is given in caption 13 in *Bath Green Park to Bristol*. (H.C.Casserley)

104.   A 1950 record of the Gloucester platforms includes the goods loop beyond platform 1. There was a subway to connect the platforms, which were used by passengers changing trains but principally, by employees of the nearby chocolate factory. There were through trains between the Midlands and Bath until 1962. (H.C.Casserley)

**Other views of this station
and those westward are
contained in our
Bath Green Park to Bristol
album.**

105.　　"Jubilee" class 4-6-0 no. 45577 *Bengal* is on the curve approaching the station with a stopping train from Gloucester to Bristol in 1958. The Ford 8 is on the dock at the east end of the goods loop. The chocolate factory had its own siding between 1912 and 1967; the building was destroyed in 1998. (R.S.Carpenter)

106.　　Class 4F no. 44523 is bound for Westerleigh Yard on 3rd April 1963, as we examine the footway to the station. The sign pointed to the subway, but did not order that it be used. (M.A.N.Johnston)

107.   Seen at the other end of the platforms on the same day is class 8F 2-8-0 no. 48737. The stone wall behind the signal was near to steps on a public footpath that passed under the junction in a second subway. The signal box had 45 levers and was destroyed by fire on 22nd January 1967, the day of total closure of the lines to Bristol. (M.A.N.Johnston)

STAPLE HILL

108.   The station was opened on 1st November 1888 to serve the developing suburban district. The 1963 eastward view includes the 518yd long tunnel, which can now be enjoyed devoid of noise and smoke. The station appears in pictures 72-76 in Bath Green Park to Bristol; it closed on 7th March 1966. (Stations UK)

FISHPONDS

XXXIV.   The 1921 edition is worthy of careful study as it reveals the diverse industries of the district. Two locomotive producers are included: Avonside (top right) and Peckett & Son (lower centre). The upper one of the two lines on the left ran to Clifton Down and carried passengers from 1st October 1874 to 1st January 1917 and from 5th May 1919 to 31st March 1941. These trains used the down bay at Fishponds. Freight continued until 14th June 1965.

109. "Stapleton" was the name used from the opening on 1st April 1866 until 1st July 1867, when it became "Fish Ponds". One word was used from 1st May 1939. The bridges and wide platforms came after the abolition of the broad gauge in 1872. The photograph is from 1963. (Stations UK)

110. The box is seen at about the same time, but it still carried two words. It had 25 levers and lasted until 12th May 1968. Sidings closed thus: Atlas Works 1959, Avonside 1953, Deep Pit and Speedwell Pit in 1936. Local goods ceased on 13th December 1965 and the station closed on 7th March 1966. (Lens of Sutton coll.)

BRISTOL ST. PHILIPS

XXXV. Our route is the upper one on the right border of this 1938 map. It passes over the GWR north of Lawrence Hill station, and runs under the street of that name before dividing. The upper line continues to the terminus at St. Philips, north of the MR goods shed. The lower line runs south and has Barrow Road Engine Shed to the left of it and Barton Hill sheds to the right of it, after passing under Day's Road. It joins GWR tracks to reach the joint station at Temple Meads, left. The tracks here are incomplete as remodelling was in progress and West of England trains were running via the St. Philips Marsh relief line on the lower part of the map. The HST depot is now on this route.

111.   The MR established its own goods depot in 1858, but shared Temple Meads with the GWR for passenger services. This became congested and so the MR built a single platform on the north side of its goods yard in 1870 for use by local trains, mainly to Bath. It closed on 21st September 1953. This 1933 photo shows that coaches had to be left in the foreground, so that the engine could be released. Closure of the goods yard took place on 1st April 1967. (Brunel University/Mowat coll.)

BARROW ROAD ENGINE SHED

112.   The shed was opened in 1873 to house MR locomotives and had a turntable at its centre, with lines radiating from it. The gas-lit interior was photographed on 5th July 1947. A carriage shed was built nearby in 1877; it lasted until 1952. (H.C.Casserley)

113.   Few photographs record the polluted atmosphere so well as this one from 24th August 1963. Featured centre are nos 45668 Madden and 73028. The tall chimney was above a furnace used for drying sand for the locomotives. We turn round for the next view. (T.Nicholls)

114.   The coaling plant was installed not long before World War II. The wagon waiting alongside it would soon be hoisted up and its contents tipped into the hopper. In the left background is Lawrence Hill Junction box, behind which are the lines from St. Philips and Avonside Wharf. The box closed on 28th July 1968. On the right is the former MR main line, which suffered a slow decline and became sidings in 1977 before being lifted. A refuse terminal was created to the left of this view in 1985. (T.Nicholls)

115.   No. 46053 is approaching Temple Meads on 2nd November 1976 with the 07.40 Leeds to Penzance. The curve on the left had been the lower part of the MR main line and the BGR's engine shed is left of centre. This was used by the MR until 1873, when the area was dedicated to wagon repairs, a task that continued here into the 1980s. An EWS diesel depot was opened here on 24th July 1995. (T.Nicholls)

BRISTOL TEMPLE MEADS

116.   LMS no. 1048 approaches the station in 1937, soon after the provision of colour light signals. The GWR was the main user of the station and so its development is studied in detail in other albums. The GWR 0-6-0PT is shunting the line leading to the goods shed and Wapping Wharf. (M.J.Tozer coll.)

117.   Most Gloucester local trains used the northern platforms, which were contained within Bristol's first station, designed by I.K.Brunel for the GWR trains from London. Standing on the centre road on 18th September 1958 is BR 2-6-2T no. 82033. This line diverged into two sidings. The platforms were numbered 13 and 14. (N.L.Browne)

118.   Moving inside the fine 1840 train shed on 23rd April 1963, we witness BR no. 75001 aiding a diseased DMU, near Old Station signal box. This closed on 12th September 1965, when all these tracks were taken out of use. The listed building remains, but ineptly in use as a car park. (T.Nicholls)

119.   From 22nd February to 20th April 1970, this track layout was simplified and resignalled, the former large east and west signal boxes being replaced by a new panel box. The platforms were also renumbered to run from north to south with the old number 1 platform on the south side being abolished. The new layout was operational on 29th April 1970 as class 52 no. D1037 *Western Empress* arrived at platform 13 (the old no.3) with the 07.06 Bradford to Penzance. Much of the old infrastructure still seemed to need updating. (G.Gillham)

> **Other views and maps of Temple Meads are in:**
> *Branch Lines around Clevedon and Portishead, Bristol to Taunton, Bristol Tramways, Frome to Bristol* **and** *Swindon to Bristol* **albums.**

120.   Until the opening of the new Post Office mail facility at Bristol Parkway, Temple Meads was the hub of the west of England mail traffic, with many trains dividing or combining here. Nos 47557 and 47491 wait with the 16.45 Plymouth-York mail, while extra vans are added to the rear of the train on 24th September 1993. (G.Gillham)

MP Middleton Press

Easebourne Lane, Midhurst, W Sussex. GU29 9AZ Tel: 01730 813169 Fax: 01730 812601
Email: sales@middletonpress.co.uk   www.middletonpress.co.uk
If books are not available from your local transport stockist, order direct post free UK.

BRANCH LINES
Branch Line to Allhallows
Branch Line to Alton
Branch Lines around Ascot
Branch Line to Ashburton
Branch Lines around Bodmin
Branch Line to Bude
Branch Lines around Canterbury
Branch Lines around Chard & Yeovil
Branch Line to Cheddar
Branch Lines around Cromer
Branch Line to the Derwent Valley
Branch Lines to East Grinstead
Branch Lines of East London
Branch Lines to Effingham Junction
Branch Lines to Enfield Town & Palace Gates
Branch Lines to Falmouth, Helston & St. Ives
Branch Line to Fairford
Branch Lines to Felixstow & Aldeburgh
Branch Lines around Gosport
Branch Line to Hayling
Branch Line to Henley, Windsor & Marlow
Branch Line to Hawkhurst
Branch Line to Horsham
Branch Lines around Huntingdon
Branch Line to Ilfracombe
Branch Line to Kingsbridge
Branch Line to Kingswear
Branch Line to Lambourn
Branch Lines to Launceston & Princetown
Branch Lines to Longmoor
Branch Lines to Looe
Branch Line to Lyme Regis
Branch Line to Lynton
Branch Lines around March
Branch Lines around Midhurst
Branch Line to Minehead
Branch Line to Moretonhampstead
Branch Lines to Newport (IOW)
Branch Lines to Newquay
Branch Lines around North Woolwich
Branch Line to Padstow
Branch Lines around Plymouth
Branch Lines to Princes Risborough
Branch Lines to Seaton and Sidmouth
Branch Lines around Sheerness
Branch Line to Shrewsbury
Branch Line to Tenterden
Branch Lines around Tiverton
Branch Lines to Torrington
Branch Lines to Tunbridge Wells
Branch Line to Upwell
Branch Line to Wantage (The Wantage Tramway)
Branch Lines of West London
Branch Lines of West Wiltshire
Branch Lines around Weymouth
Branch Lines around Wimborne
Branch Lines around Wisbech

NARROW GAUGE
Austrian Narrow Gauge
Branch Line to Lynton
Branch Lines around Portmadoc 1923-46
Branch Lines around Porthmadog 1954-94
Branch Line to Southwold
Douglas to Port Erin
Douglas to Peel
Kent Narrow Gauge
Northern France Narrow Gauge
Romneyrail
Sierra Leone Narrow Gauge
Southern France Narrow Gauge
Sussex Narrow Gauge
Surrey Narrow Gauge

Swiss Narrow Gauge
Two-Foot Gauge Survivors
Vivarais Narrow Gauge

SOUTH COAST RAILWAYS
Ashford to Dover
Bournemouth to Weymouth
Brighton to Eastbourne
Brighton to Worthing
Dover to Ramsgate
Eastbourne to Hastings
Hastings to Ashford
Ryde to Ventnor
Southampton to Bournemouth

SOUTHERN MAIN LINES
Basingstoke to Salisbury
Crawley to Littlehampton
Dartford to Sittingbourne
East Croydon to Three Bridges
Epsom to Horsham
Exeter to Barnstaple
Exeter to Tavistock
London Bridge to East Croydon
Tonbridge to Hastings
Salisbury to Yeovil
Sittingbourne to Ramsgate
Swanley to Ashford
Tavistock to Plymouth
Three Bridges to Brighton
Victoria to Bromley South
Victoria to East Croydon
Waterloo to Windsor
Waterloo to Woking
Woking to Portsmouth
Woking to Southampton
Yeovil to Exeter

EASTERN MAIN LINES
Barking to Southend
Ely to Kings Lynn
Ely to Norwich
Fenchurch Street to Barking
Hitchin to Peterborough
Ilford to Shenfield
Ipswich to Saxmundham
Liverpool Street to Ilford
Saxmundham to Yarmouth
Tilbury Loop

WESTERN MAIN LINES
Banbury to Birmingham
Bristol to Taunton
Didcot to Banbury
Didcot to Swindon
Ealing to Slough
Exeter to Newton Abbot
Moreton-in-Marsh to Worcester
Newton Abbot to Plymouth
Newbury to Westbury
Oxford to Moreton-in-Marsh
Paddington to Ealing
Paddington to Princes Risborough
Plymouth to St. Austell
Princes Risborough to Banbury
Reading to Didcot
Slough to Newbury
St. Austell to Penzance
Swindon to Bristol
Swindon to Newport
Taunton to Exeter
Westbury to Taunton

MIDLAND MAIN LINES
Bedford to Wellingborough
Euston to Harrow & Wealdstone
Gloucester to Bristol
Harrow to Watford
St. Albans to Bedford
St. Pancras to St. Albans

COUNTRY RAILWAY ROUTES
Abergavenny to Merthyr
Andover to Southampton
Bath to Evercreech Junction
Bath Green Park to Bristol
Bournemouth to Evercreech Junction
Brecon to Newport
Burnham to Evercreech Junction
Cheltenham to Andover
Croydon to East Grinstead
Didcot to Winchester
East Kent Light Railway
Fareham to Salisbury
Frome to Bristol
Guildford to Redhill
Reading to Basingstoke
Reading to Guildford
Redhill to Ashford
Salisbury to Westbury
Stratford upon Avon to Cheltenham
Strood to Paddock Wood
Taunton to Barnstaple
Wenford Bridge to Fowey
Westbury to Bath
Woking to Alton
Yeovil to Dorchester

GREAT RAILWAY ERAS
Ashford from Steam to Eurostar
Festiniog in the Fifties
Festiniog in the Sixties
Festiniog 50 years of enterprise
Isle of Wight Lines 50 years of change
Railways to Victory 1944-46
Return to Blaenau 1970-82
SECR Centenary album
Talyllyn 50 years of change
Wareham to Swanage 50 years of change
Yeovil 50 years of change

LONDON SUBURBAN RLYS
Caterham and Tattenham Corner
Charing Cross to Dartford
Clapham Jn. to Beckenham Jn.
Crystal Palace (HL) & Catford Loop
East London Line
Finsbury Park to Alexandra Palace
Holborn Viaduct to Lewisham
Kingston and Hounslow Loops
Lewisham to Dartford
Lines around Wimbledon
Liverpool Street to Chingford
Mitcham Junction Lines
North London Line
South London Line
West Croydon to Epsom
West London Line
Willesden Junction to Richmond
Wimbledon to Beckenham
Wimbledon to Epsom

STEAMING THROUGH
Steaming through Cornwall
Steaming through the Isle of Wight
Steaming through Kent
Steaming through West Hants

TRAMWAY CLASSICS
Aldgate & Stepney Tramways
Barnet & Finchley Tramways
Bath Tramways
Brighton's Tramways
Bristol's Tramways
Burton & Ashby Tramways
Camberwell & W.Norwood Tramways
Clapham & Streatham Tramways
Croydon's Tramways
Derby Tramways
Dover's Tramways
East Ham & West Ham Tramways
Edgware and Willesden Tramways
Eltham & Woolwich Tramways
Exeter & Taunton Tramways
Fulwell - Home to Trams, Trolleys and Buses
Great Yarmouth Tramways
Greenwich & Dartford Tramways
Hammersmith & Hounslow Tramways
Hampstead & Highgate Tramways
Holborn & Finsbury Tramways
Ilford & Barking Tramways
Kingston & Wimbledon Tramways
Lewisham & Catford Tramways
Liverpool Tramways 1. Eastern Routes
Liverpool Tramways 2. Southern Routes
Liverpool Tramways 3. Northern Routes
Maidstone & Chatham Tramways
Margate to Ramsgate
North Kent Tramways
Norwich Tramways
Reading Tramways
Shepherds Bush & Uxbridge Tramways
Southend-on-sea Tramways
South London Line Tramways 1903-33
Southwark & Deptford Tramways
Stamford Hill Tramways
Twickenham & Kingston Tramways
Victoria & Lambeth Tramways
Waltham Cross & Edmonton Tramways
Walthamstow & Leyton Tramways
Wandsworth & Battersea Tramways

TROLLEYBUS CLASSICS
Bradford Trolleybuses
Croydon Trolleybuses
Darlington Trolleybuses
Derby Trolleybuses
Huddersfield Trolleybuses
Hull Trolleybuses
Portsmouth Trolleybuses
Reading Trolleybuses

WATERWAY & SHIPPING
Kent and East Sussex Waterways
London to Portsmouth Waterway
Sussex Shipping - Sail, Steam & Motor
West Sussex Waterways

MILITARY BOOKS
Battle over Portsmouth
Battle over Sussex 1940
Blitz over Sussex 1941-42
Bombers over Sussex 1943-45
Bognor at War
East Ridings Secret Resistance
Military Defence of West Sussex
Military Signals from the South Coast
Secret Sussex Resistance
Sussex Home Guard
Surrey Home Guard

OTHER RAILWAY BOOKS
Collectors for Trains, Trolleys & Trams
Industrial Railways of the South-East
South Eastern & Chatham Railways
London Chatham & Dover Railway
London Termini - Past and Proposed
War on the Line (SR 1939-45)